EVERYDAY MODIFICATIONS FOR YOUR

MORRIS MINOR

EVERYDAY MODIFICATIONS FOR YOUR

MORRIS MINOR

MATT TOMKINS

THE CROWOOD PRESS

First published in 2023 by
The Crowood Press Ltd
Ramsbury, Marlborough
Wiltshire SN8 2HR

enquiries@crowood.com

www.crowood.com

British Library Cataloguing-in-Publication Data
A catalogue record for this book is available from the British Library.

ISBN 978 0 7198 4197 2

Dedication
It would not have been possible to produce this book without the help and support of a great many people over a number of years. Friendship has surrounded my involvement with these little cars, and there are too many people to mention in my journey from learner driver through to motoring journalist who have shaped me, taught me and inspired me. This book is the culmination of twelve years' advice received and errors made. I must thank everyone who has contributed images, or allowed me to photograph their car for this book. I must also thank my wonderful wife, Emmy, for putting up with my endless hours of scribbling, researching and spanner-spinning during the production of this title.

Photographic acknowledgements
The majority of the pictures in this book were taken by the author or Tom Critchell. The author would like to thank the following for supplying the other images, as follows: Andrew Clark, pp. 59 and 98 (bottom); Andrew Curran, p.112; ESM Morris Minors, pp.12, 20, 22, 29, 30, 53 (left), 61 (middle right), 62 (top right), 63 (top), 74 (left, both), 79 (bottom), 80, 81 (bottom), 85 (top left), 90, 97, 104, 105 (bottom) and 120 (right); Stephen Gordon , p.60; JLH Morris Minors, pp.86 (middle) and 98 (top); Longstone Tyres, p.68; Machine Mart, p.9; Andrew Bywater, Mirabelle Classic Cars, p.61; Ethan Morris, p.114 (right); Newton Commercial, p.113; Nuffield Organisation, pp.49 (right) and 76; Retronics (p.121); Chris Ryder, pp.62 (left), 62 (bottom), 82 (top left) and 86 (middle); Luke Tomkins, pp.85 and 86; and Brian Wood, p.61 (left).

Typeset by Chennai Publishing Services

Cover design by Blue Sunflower Creative

Printed and bound in India by Replika Press Pvt Ltd

Contents

Part I: The Basics

Introduction

Drive a Morris Minor and the world seems a happier place. People on the street smile as you parp past, and you will strike up conversations with strangers every time you fill the tank with petrol. You attract cheery waves from other road users and, whether you remember these cars in use in their own period or not, the sense of nostalgia for a time gone by is enormous.

Limiting the use of your Morris Minor only to trips to classic car shows or Sunday picnics, then, would be to miss out on a huge amount of potential pleasure and enjoyment. However, the world has changed since the Minor was ubiquitous on Britain's roads, with higher speeds and greater volume of traffic on the road, so using a Minor regularly in its standard form can present some challenges and require certain compromises.

Many of these compromises were addressed to some extent by the manufacturer throughout the car's impressive 23-year production span. Indeed, the Minor outlived the Riley One-Point-Five and Wolseley 1500 Models that were intended to replace it, and it was not until the introduction of the Morris Marina (itself mechanically very similar to the Minor and therefore the victim over the years of much parts pillaging), that the Minor's reign as the British-built family car of choice came to an end.

Unveiled on 27 October 1948 at the British Motor Show held at Earl's Court, Series MM 'lowlight' Minors and the earliest 'high light' cars were fitted with sidevalve engines and a number of other running gear components carried over from the pre-war Morris 8 Series E, built between 1938 and 1948. There will not be much focus on these very early cars in this book, as their numbers are relatively limited now and they are unlikely to be modified for daily use, given their historic significance. That said, much of what follows will be applicable to these cars with some detail changes, which we will explore in brief later in this book.

In 1952, the Morris Minor received a major re-work for the Series II. The sidevalve engine was replaced by the now ubiquitous A-series (in 803cc form), and much of the running gear was updated, from which all later variations evolved. The introduction of the 948cc A-series engine, accompanied by the 'Minor 1000' moniker and numerous other drivetrain alterations in 1956 coincided with the dawn of the motorway era and was intended to keep the Minor relevant in that modern era which continues to this day.

The final significant change to the Minor's drivetrain came in 1962, with the Series V cars. A 1098cc A-series engine replaced the 948cc unit with larger drum brakes (seven inches increased to eight), improved gearbox and taller final drive, making this the most usable of all of the factory-original Morris Minors on 21st-century roads.

The Minor is blessed with an incredibly strong aftermarket parts supply from a number of specialists, an active owners club and many specialist businesses with a wealth of knowledge when it comes to maintaining and modifying these cars. There is a precedent for most modifications possible on the Minor and so seeking advice or specialist assistance should not prove too difficult.

The Morris Minor Owners Club (MMOC) organises events throughout the year, including its infamous Minors On Tour (European) and Minors On Tour UK events, both of which are focused on useability over originality. You will not be chased off the rally field for upgrading your engine or brakes – rather, you will be joining a band of enthusiasts for whom enabling the continued everyday enjoyment of the cars which the club celebrates is as important as preserving low-mileage original cars with crossply tyres and seven-inch drum brakes. Indeed, at the time of writing, the Chairman of the MMOC owns and drives a 1275-propelled Traveller with a five-speed gearbox, the Secretary's low-light tourer has an aftermarket Alta cylinder head fitted to its sidevalve engine and the Webmaster runs a splendid modified Traveller with a rather highly strung 1380 A+ under its bonnet.

Alongside its own club and marque specialists, the Minor also benefits from the overarching umbrella that is the wider BMC and BL family of models. The Morris Marina, MG Midget, Mini, ADO16s, Wolseley 1500 and Riley One-Point-Five, Austin A35s and A40s and more all yield parts and knowledge both from their own development story and subsequent use and modification which can be used to develop your Morris Minor. Many of these interchangeable parts are in good supply thanks to strong enthusiast bases for these classics, so sourcing upgrades for your Minor which are standard parts for an MG Midget or Mini, for example, should provide no problem at all.

In this book, we will look into a number of sensible everyday modifications that you can make to your own Morris Minor, or look for in a prospective purchase, which will serve to make the car more usable on the roads of today. These range from upgrading engines, gearboxes and brakes with components from within the Morris Minor's own evolution to seeking parts and inspiration from elsewhere within the BMC range and beyond. We will also explore the wealth of aftermarket parts, accessories and expertise which makes modifying the Morris Minor a well-trodden path with myriad options available to you, depending on your own needs and desires.

Many of the bolt-on modifications that we will cover are supplied with detailed instructions for their fitting when purchased from specialist suppliers, so we will be introducing you to the pros and cons of these modifications and when and why you might need them, rather than providing detailed step-by-step instructions in every case, as kits can change and evolve and our advice may well be out of date by the time you read this. We will, however, be covering in more detail some of the tweaks and adjustments, such as lowering the suspension ride height, which you can do at home without the need to purchase any bolt-on components.

Do not think of what follows as a list of modifications that should all be done immediately. In fact, we will start by asking the question as to whether you need to upgrade at all, working through common service tasks and seeking to ensure that you are starting from a good basis before using modifications as sticking plaster solutions to mask the effects of disrepair. We will also ask at each juncture exactly what it is you want your Minor to be. Are you looking for a B-road bumbler or a motorway mile-muncher? Because the approaches you will need to take in each case will differ considerably.

The following advice, then, is intended less as a set menu, but more as a guided tour of a buffet. In this, we will explore which flavours work well together to produce the ultimate Morris Minor sandwich. We will also take a brief wander to the far end of the table where we will find the olives, Stinking Bishop cheese and anchovies as we take a look at some more radical modifications which, despite their bold flavours, may only appeal to a few people's palettes.

Once we have familiarised ourselves with the selection of ingredients on offer, we will glance at a few plates put together by experienced Morris Minor chefs, through a series of road tests to see what flavour combinations work well together. Just as in the case of chilli and chocolate, there may well be a few surprises along the way…

1

Safety

Everything in this book is intended as guidance, not as specific instructions, and it is your responsibility to ensure that you are working safely and that you are competent enough to complete work on your car both in a safe manner and to a safe standard. Working on a car carries risks, and it is also your responsibility to identify and mitigate these risks. If you are not confident in doing a job yourself, what follows in this book will still be a useful guide to allow you to commission a specialist, garage or mobile mechanic to carry out the work for you.

Always carry out due diligence when it comes to choosing someone to work on your Minor. Seek recommendations from other owners who have used the company or individual for work in the past and inspect examples of previous work carefully. Be sure to get quotes for the cost of any work up front and in writing and ask to be kept informed as the project develops.

It is important to say at this point that there is no such thing as a stupid question. If you are unsure about any aspect of working on your car, especially something safety-critical, it pays to ask for advice. Whether you choose to attend a course on vehicle maintenance (there are several available, including lectures and workshops days at the British Motor Museum, Gaydon, and short courses though the Heritage Skills Academy based at Bicester Heritage), or you can simply join your local branch of the Morris Minor Owners Club. Advice is readily on hand from a variety of sources with a growing desire within the classic car community to share skills and keep the hobby alive in an ever more digital-focused world.

Alongside your spanners, screwdrivers and socket sets should sit safety goggles, gloves, steel toe-capped boots, and masks, all of which should be worn where appropriate. It is also worthwhile equipping your workshop with a fire extinguisher of appropriate size and type for the work being undertaken. An extinguisher and leather welding gauntlets are also a worthwhile addition to your Minor, in an easily accessible place, to allow you to tackle a fire out on the road – if it is safe to do so – before it takes hold.

SAFE LIFTING

In almost any aspect of maintaining or modifying your Morris Minor, you will need to raise and support the car for access to the underside or to enable the removal of

Achieving altitude is essential for most tasks. However, extreme care must be taken to ensure the car cannot fall on you.

Factory-supplied jack is flimsy and relies on the jacking point being perfectly solid. Its use is not recommended.

Bottle jacks are compact enough to keep below the boot floor and lift in a fixed vertical plane.

A quality trolley jack is essential for workshop tasks. Aluminium items as pictured offer a great advantage in reduced weight.

Smaller trolley jacks may be carried in the car for roadside repairs. Folding axle stands and chocks are also available for this purpose.

suspension components. Doing so safely is crucial and care must be taken to assess the risks involved from the outset.

The first and most important piece of advice is NEVER to work beneath a car supported only by a jack. Axle stands, properly and securely positioned, are essential when it

A quality set of axle stands is essential. Never get under a car supported only on a jack.

Strengthened tie rod mounts on the chassis legs make ideal jacking points.

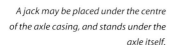

A jack may be placed under the centre of the axle casing, and stands under the axle itself.

comes to working on any car. Jacks and axle stands should be carefully inspected before each use to ensure that they are in good condition, jack hydraulics are not leaking, frameworks are not bent, and welds inspected for cracking or failure. Of course, all jacking equipment should be sufficiently weight-rated, too.

If you choose to use drive-on car ramps, inspect these carefully as well and ensure that they are anchored before attempting to drive onto them, as these ramps can easily slip forward. Ensure you use a spotter to ensure you are driving onto the ramps squarely and that you stop before over-running the stop. Always use a secondary set

of supports (for example, axle stands) beneath the car when using drive-on ramps, too, to catch the car in the event of ramp failure. The higher the drive-on ramp, the more difficult it will be to drive onto it. Consider investing in a set of hydraulically operated self-raising ramps, which allow a good raised height to be achieved without the need to drive up a steep sloping ramp. These are ideal for lowered cars which could foul their bumpers on steeper ramps.

If you intend to undertake a large amount of work on your Minor, and your budget and workspace allow, you may consider investing in a centre-rise scissor lift, or even a commercial-style two- or four-post lift. These certainly make work much easier; however, financially they are beyond the reach of most home mechanics so, for the most part, when discussing the processes involved in certain maintenance and modification procedures, we will assume that you are working on axle stands in a private garage or driveway. Rollover jigs and rotisseries are especially helpful for restoration work, and have reduced in price significantly in recent years. There is also a buoyant second-hand market for such items, as they are bulky to store once a restoration for which they were originally purchased has been completed.

The Minor's factory-supplied jack (apart from on very early cars or vans which had jacking points positioned on front and rear inner wings) fits into the jacking points on each end of the central cross-member. These jacking points are notorious rot spots, so an original jack should only be used if the jacking point's condition is known to be excellent, and even then, only really in an emergency for changing a wheel and such like. Instruction on how to use the original-style jack can be found in the original factory operation manual.

A good quality trolley jack, then, is a sound investment, as are a pair of good quality axle stands. Choose a good quality set-up from a trusted supplier. Cheap imitations of older designs might appear to be an online bargain, but the material and construction quality can leave much to be desired, with reports of weld and hydraulic failures early in service life quite commonplace. A small portable jack should be more than up to most tasks; however, a larger jack with a wider base size and a higher lift will be more useful, and is the safest option, so one of these is a sound investment if your storage space and budget allow. Lightweight aluminium versions of these larger jacks – originally designed for racing teams that require maximum portability – are becoming increasingly affordable for the home user. They are well worth considering if moving a heavy steel jack around your workspace lacks appeal.

Bottle or scissor jacks are useful for keeping in the boot of the car for on the road repairs such as replacing a wheel, and can be neatly stowed alongside (or inside, in the case of some smaller screw-type jacks) the spare wheel under the boot floor, while folding axle stands are available which make a great addition to a tool kit for running repairs while touring. It pays to keep an offcut of hardwood in the boot as well, to spread the load of a jack on the underbody of the car. To prevent unwanted rattles and damage to paintwork, it is worth wrapping these boot-stowed jack and stands in rags or an offcut of carpet and securing them where possible.

When positioning either a jack or axle stands, first it is important to establish that the vehicle structure onto which they are to be positioned is in good, solid condition. The ground onto which the jack or stand is to be placed should be solid and level, and consideration should be given to the weight distribution, centre of balance and the areas of the car to which access will be required. Also note whether a task will need the suspension to be in droop or compression, as the positioning of jacks and supports will differ. Finally, consider whether a task (such as removing the engine) may change the centre of balance mid-way through a job and render the car unstable.

Raising the front

At the front of the car, the best jacking point is the strengthened portion of the chassis legs where the tie rod mounts. Raising the car from here allows the suspension to droop and an axle stand to be positioned further back along the chassis leg. If the suspension needs to be compressed, a jack may be positioned beneath the lower wishbones, but care must be taken to avoid the jack slipping when the angle of the suspension component changes as the car is raised/lowered.

Raising the rear

At the back, the centre of the axle casing makes for the strongest jacking point, and allows both sides of the car to be raised simultaneously. With the car raised in this fashion, axle stands may be placed either side of the axle, although care must be taken to avoid damaging the brake lines as the car is lowered onto the stands. If the suspension is required to be in droop, axle stands may be placed just behind the rear spring hangers and the jack lowered to allow the rear leaf springs to become uncompressed.

ELECTRICAL SAFETY

Before commencing any work on your Morris Minor, it pays to get into the habit of disconnecting the battery, as an electrical short can endanger both you and your Minor's wiring loom. Never place parts or tools on top of your Minor's battery (tempting as it is, located at the rear of the engine bay at a convenient height) as a direct short circuit between the two battery terminals could result in explosion, fire and/or leak of acid from the battery.

Always disconnect the battery earth terminal first, and reconnect it last. This way, should your spanner touch the bodywork or battery clamp while tightening the live terminal, the circuit is not completed and a dead short is avoided. Similarly, if the spanner being used to tighten the earth lead touches the body of the car, that side of the circuit is already connected together, so there is no harm done.

A battery cut-off is a useful upgrade to prevent the need for the battery to be continually disconnected for work, and also offers a quick and easy way of disconnecting the car's power in the event of a fire or as an additional security measure. We will cover fitting a battery cut-off and the various types of this item that are available in Chapter 12.

FUEL SAFETY

Petrol, by its very nature, is extremely volatile, and so care must be taken to ensure that sources of ignition or heat are kept away from any pools of petrol, fuel lines and tank. Inspect the entirety of your fuel system regularly and thoroughly for leaks or deterioration and rectify any issues as a matter of urgency. Don't forget to inspect the fuel filler neck to tank pipe and the condition of the cork gasket where the fuel level sender mounts into the top of the tank. We will discuss hose specifications recommended when using modern fuels in Chapter 2.

Never weld near fuel lines or the fuel tank. It is a straight-forward enough, if time-consuming, job to remove a Minor's fuel tank and drain down the carburettor and fuel lines if major welding work is to be undertaken. A drain plug is positioned on the bottom of the petrol tank; how-ever, it is recommended that the tank is removed com-pletely from the vehicle before hot work is undertaken in its proximity, as an empty tank can still explode if exposed to a source of ignition due to the vapours which will remain inside. Never attempt to weld a fuel tank. Replacements are available in standard and large-capacity forms, brand new for a modest cost and well worth the investment, given the dangers associated with attempting a welded repair on a tank that has been already exposed to petrol.

Fuel tanks are available brand new and not as expensive as you might think. Well worth the investment over risking a dangerous repair.

WORKING ON BRAKES

Failure to accomplish engine work successfully can be frustrating, but failure to stop is far more dangerous than a failure to proceed. If you are to embark on working on your Minor's brakes, it is critical that you are competent in doing so and that all work carried out is to the highest of standards with the best available components.

One of the most common points of failure in a hydraulic system is fluid leaking around an incorrectly flared union. This can be avoided by purchasing, at very modest cost, pre-made brake lines for the areas to be disturbed (or a complete kit), which are pre-cut to the required lengths and have professionally fitted flares and brand new unions of the correct thread diameter and pitch already fitted.

After disturbing the hydraulic system, it pays to check very carefully for leaks once the job is complete and the system bled. Ask an assistant to sit in the driver's seat and apply pressure to the brake pedal. It should not sink. If it does, either there is a leak in the system or failure of the internal seals within the master cylinder. If it takes a few pumps of the pedal to establish a firm pedal, but no sinking occurs thereafter, suspect air in the system and re-bleed.

With constant pressure applied to the brake pedal, carefully inspect all unions with a torch for leakage and rectify any issues found immediately and before taking the car on the road. Like most cars of its era, the Minor employs a single circuit braking system, meaning that all of the brakes are operated by the same master cylinder. In the event of master cylinder failure or a fluid leak from either a pipe, union or slave cylinder (or caliper, in the case of cars upgraded to disc brakes), total brake failure may occur. It is therefore essential that the brak-ing system is maintained to the highest order, including the handbrake, which also serves as an emergency brake should fluid pressure be lost.

HAZARDOUS SUBSTANCES

Brake dust, paint fumes, exhaust gases and engine oil all carry their own health risks, as do many other substances and processes associated with car repair, modification and maintenance, and as such it is essential that safety meas-ures are taken to mitigate their impact.

Very old braking or clutch components may contain asbestos in the friction material and, although sale of such components as replacement parts is now banned under

Never blow away brake dust, always clean it down wet; it can be hazardous to health.

Acceptable changes.

REACH (UK Registration, Evaluation, Authorisation and restriction of CHemicals) legislation, your Morris Minor may still be fitted with such linings and appropriate care must be taken to mitigate risks while working on these systems. Never blow away brake or clutch dust – always damp it down either with soapy water or brake and clutch cleaner.

Petrol is volatile by its very nature and oils, brake fluid and battery acid are all hazardous both to health and to the environment. Therefore, they should always be disposed of in the correct manner. If in any doubt, consult your local council on the best methods and locations for disposal of hazardous materials in your area.

INSURANCE, MOTS AND HISTORIC INTEREST

It is important to take note that any modifications you make to your Morris Minor should be declared to your insurance company. Failure to do so could result in a claim being refused, and potentially a legal battle on your hands in the event of an accident. Even if you feel an upgrade is for safety's sake rather than performance, it must be declared. Transparency is by far the best policy and any increase in premium will be far less than the cost of a refused claim.

The good news is that there is a precedent for almost every modification possible to the Morris Minor (and certainly for everything covered in this book), and most specialist classic insurers will be more than happy to take note of any changes from standard specification with very little increase in premium.

At the time of writing, any car built more than 40 years ago is defined as a 'Vehicle of Historic Interest' and does not require, by law, an MOT test unless 'substantially changed' in the past 30 years. Take some time to study the definition of substantial changes here: https://www.gov.uk/government/publications/historic-classic-vehicles-mot-exemption-criteria.

Guidance on what are considered acceptable changes can be found in the image above taken from the Department for Transport website.

This ruling came about in response to an EU directive on roadworthiness through the work of the Federation of British Historic Vehicle Clubs (FBHVC) and the body's continued work to ensure unhindered use of historic vehicles on the roads of tomorrow. The Federation's website offers up-to-date information about MOT exemption, fuels and more and is well worth a read. Click to www.fbhvc.co.uk

Almost all of the modifications and upgrades which will be discussed in the following pages, including engine changes within the 'A-series family', fall into either of two categories of acceptable change. Either they are *changes of a type which can be demonstrated to have been made when vehicles of the type were in production or within ten years of the end of production,*' or '*axles and running gear have been changed to improve efficiency, safety or environmental performance.*'

Later chapters will briefly discuss upgrading to more modern engines, which could result in the car falling outside of the MOT exemption criteria. However, it is the opinion of the author that submitting your Morris Minor, whether modified or not, for a voluntary MOT test with a tester who is familiar with the age of the car is a good idea. At the very least, an MOT test gives the opportunity for a second, independent pair of eyes to check your handiwork. It's all too easy to become 'snow blind' when working on your own car.

2

Morris Minors and Modern Fuels

The liquid chemistry of the petrol on sale when the Minor was designed and built was significantly different to what is on sale today. There is no need to panic, though, as with a little knowledge, a few tweaks and a keen eye, there is every reason to continue using pump petrol in your Minor for many years to come.

UNLEADED PETROL

When the Morris Minor was first built, the petrol with which it was designed to be filled contained a substance called 'tetraethyl lead'. Tetraethyl lead was originally added to petrol in the 1920s in order to prevent pre-ignition or 'pinking' under load. However, it was also found to offer lubrication and protection to the top end of the engine, including protecting valves and cast-iron valve seats from being burned and damaged.

By 1989, however, a change to unleaded petrol was seen as inevitable, with research proving links between lead pollution and brain damage in children. *Autocar* magazine reported in 1989 that the UK was pumping three thousand tonnes of the stuff into the atmosphere every year.

Modern fuels need not be a cause for concern with a little diligence.

Pump petrol should still be available well into the future.

Under EU rules at the start of 2000, lead was removed from standard pump petrol in Britain. This raised great concern in the classic car community, with many fearing that their classics would suffer irreparable damage by using the new unleaded petrol. Lead replacement additives were made available by a number of suppliers and many owners removed cylinder heads to fit hardened valve seats. These prevented the risk of burning original valve seats that were cut directly into the cast cylinder head in order to cope with the unleaded fuel.

The Federation of British Historic Vehicle Clubs (FBHVC) has conducted a great deal of research into the subject, the conclusions of which can be found on their website at www.fbhvc.co.uk. For our purposes, however, in the present day, we must only consider the cylinder head in respect of the effect of the removal of lead from petrol, and the potential damage that may be caused to the valve seats by its use. Of course, different octane ratings and volatility will also have an effect on the running of the vehicle, but in the present day we will cover these as service adjustments rather than a transition from leaded to unleaded fuel.

So What Can Be Done?

Additives such as Valvemaster Plus or Tetraboost may be used to protect against the effect of unleaded fuel on classic car cylinder heads. However, many owners choose to fit hardened valve seats to the cylinder head to allow the use of modern fuel without an additive. In order to modify a cylinder head to be suitable for use with unleaded fuel, first it needs to be removed from the engine. Luckily, in the case of the Morris Minor this process is incredibly straightforward and can be undertaken within an hour by a competent home mechanic with just a few tools.

At this point you may choose to strip and inspect the cylinder head yourself, removing valves, checking for play in the valve guides necessitating replacement and checking valve springs for any signs of damage, before sending the bare casting to a machine shop to have hardened valve seats fitted and cut. Alternatively, you may choose to send the cylinder head complete to the machine shop for them to undertake the work as a whole. Note that new valves will need to be fitted at the same time, as will new valve stem oil seals, and it is a good idea to have the 'head checked for flatness and skimmed to remove any distortion at the same time. It may be more cost- and time-effective, if you are not set on keeping the original cylinder head for your car, to simply exchange your original cylinder head for one already converted on an exchange basis from one of the many specialist suppliers for the Morris Minor.

Of course, there are also those who simply choose to use unleaded fuel with neither an unleaded converted cylinder head or lead additive, and whose circumstantial evidence proves at least in many cases that the resilient A-series engine can be run for many miles without issue. Many take the view that 'if and when a valve seat is burned, then is the time to remove the cylinder head and fit hardened valve seats using the cash saved from not using additives.'

The choice is yours, then, as to the course of action which you feel most comfortable taking, but also bear in mind that your Minor may well have been fitted with hardened valve seats before your ownership. Check any paperwork carefully for evidence of this or, if it is removed for any other reason, inspect the underside of the cylinder head around the valves for evidence of a hardened seat having been fitted.

E10 – A Ticking Time Bomb?

A more recent change to the liquid chemistry of the petrol we in the UK use to fill our tanks came in September 2021, when the ethanol content of standard grade pump petrol was raised from between zero and five per cent (known as E5) to between five and ten per cent (known as E10), this change having been rolled out across Europe since 2009, and caveated with warnings that many vehicles built before 2011 may not be suitable for use with the new fuel.

Once again we can turn to the work of the FBHVC, who are continually updating their website with a great deal of information, research and advice on the subject of fuels, as well as lobbying parliament for the continued unrestricted use of older vehicles.

At the time of writing, the continued availability of a protection grade E5 fuel seems highly likely for the foreseeable future. When the change came in, in September 2021, the government legislated that for at least five years (the maximum permissible term for such legislation by law) E5 must continue to be offered as an option by retailers who sell over a million litres of petrol per year. Look for the E5 label on the pump and an octane rating of 97 and above. For those seeking to use their Minors without modifications to suit ethanol-blended fuels, you will be interested to know that at the time of writing Esso states on its website that its Supreme+99 petrol contains no ethanol at all (falling within the zero to five per cent criteria for E5 labelling). The Esso website states: 'Although our pumps have E5 labels on them, our Synergy Supreme+ 99 is actually ethanol free

'Protection grade' E5 must be provided by law thanks to the work of the FBHVC.

(except, due to technical supply reasons, in Devon, Cornwall, North Wales, North England and Scotland).' Source: www.esso.co.uk/en-gb/fuels/petrol.

It should be noted that using ethanol-free petrol does not negate the need for due diligence, with regular and careful checks to fuel lines remaining an essential part of day-to-day maintenance.

When questioned in 2021 on the issue of continued availability of E5 after the 2026 end of the current protection grade legislation, FBHVC chairman David Whale told the author:

> *The Federation are confident that, unless a suitable alternative becomes available, the government will continue to legislate for the provision of a protection grade fuel for use in older cars for the foreseeable future… Classic owners can help the case for continued provision by continuing to use this protection grade fuel in their cars, proving a demand to retailers and legislators.*

The problems

Ethanol is hygroscopic, meaning that it actively attracts moisture. This can be a problem if your car is laid up for long periods, as water absorbed from the air mixes with the ethanol in the fuel to make a weak acid which can cause corrosion to steel fuel tanks. There are advantages to this hygroscopic property of ethanol-blended fuels. If any moisture is present in the bottom of your Minor's petrol tank, it will be absorbed and burned, removing it from the tank and reducing the chance of corrosion of the fuel tank. Dry fuel water-removal additives often used in marine applications work on this same principle.

Ethanol is also a strong solvent. It can therefore dissolve previously dormant dirt and detritus from the bottom of your Morris Minor's fuel tank and the walls of the fuel lines. As a strong solvent, ethanol can attack rubber fuel lines and gaskets, which must be replaced for ethanol-resistant (R9) alternatives as well as carburettor floats and solder. Read on to find out how these problems can be resolved.

The solutions

It is possible to convert your Morris Minor for use with E10 fuel relatively simply. This is at least for safety's sake for fill-ups when E5 'protection grade' petrol is unavailable. Starting from the front and working back, carburettor floats can be replaced with StayUp versions manufactured by Burlen SU. From standard, the Minor uses the ubiquitous HS-type float on all but very early models with H-type carburettors, which will use either the 1.5 inch T1 float or 1-inch diameter T2 float. Modified cars may use HIF floats. A comprehensive range of these military-grade closed cell floats which promise to be resistant to modern ethanol-based fuels is available at www.sucarb.co.uk.

While we are in the float chamber, an upgraded viton-tipped needle valve is a sensible upgrade, and should be replaced in the course of general carburettor maintenance, as should the jet assembly and its o-ring (a common leak-point), where it joins the float chamber. These o-rings are integral to the jet assembly and modern replacements are manufactured from rubber compatible with modern fuels. If you suspect that your Morris Minor is still fitted with its original jet assembly, this is a job which should be high up your priority list, as a leak here will drip fuel onto the hot exhaust manifold with potentially catastrophic consequences.

Working back, the rubber fuel line that connects the petrol pump to the carburettor float chamber must be replaced with a hose to specification SAE J30 R9 and inspected regularly. As with the jet-to-float chamber o-ring, a leak here will likely cause fuel to drip onto the hot exhaust manifold, which is distinctly inadvisable. The author recommends not using metal braided fuel hoses which, although aesthetically pleasing in a nicely detailed engine bay, cannot be easily inspected and often a leak is the first sign of failure, by which time discovery may come too late. It is also sensible to fit an in-line fuel filter to this pipe, which will serve to catch debris dislodged by the solvent properties of the ethanol from the fuel tank and lines.

The fuel pump itself is another potential point of failure, due to exposure to ethanol-based fuel. Older diaphragms may stretch or perish when exposed to E10. Rebuild kits are available – as are complete replacement pumps, which are E10-ready – either direct from Burlen or via your usual specialist Morris Minor parts suppliers.

The main tank-to-pump metal fuel line is unlikely to present much of an issue, although soldered joints where the unions meet the pipes may eventually succumb to the effects of ethanol, which can attack soft solder resulting in

a failure of the joint. As this pipe is on the unpressurised side of the system, a leak is likely to be a dribble rather than a gush. It is worth paying careful attention to the soldered joints at both ends of the main fuel line and, should an issue arise, consider replacing the pipe in its entirety with a copper-nickel replacement that uses flared ends, as offered by Automec via many of the Morris Minor parts suppliers. This does away with the soldered joints entirely, and replacement of this line is a straightforward enough task, the most difficult part being forming the swan-neck shape where the pipe meets the fuel pump. This is best done using a proprietary pipe-forming tool or a baked bean tin as a former and carefully drawing the pipe into shape.

The petrol tank itself is made from steel and can corrode. The problem of ethanol being hygroscopic in its nature and so absorbing water from the air can be mitigated in a variety of ways. If E10 fuel is left in the tank for a long period of time, moisture can be sucked from the air in the tank and through the vented breather in the fuel cap, sink to the bottom of the tank, and cause corrosion. This problem can be mitigated, of course, by using low- or no-ethanol fuels, either super unleaded containing between zero and five per cent ethanol or ethanol-free storage fuel from specialist suppliers for the last few tanks prior to winter storage, while keeping petrol tanks full prevents the risk of condensation within a tank. It is also worthwhile blocking the tank breather over winter to prevent moisture from the air being drawn in. Alternatively, constant use keeps the fuel flowing through the tank and minimises the opportunity for water to precipitate out of the petrol and cause corrosion. In fact, higher ethanol content in fuel means that if the car is in constant use, any water which has made its way into the tank over the course of the car's life will be absorbed by the hygroscopic fuel and burned.

If corrosion has taken hold in your fuel tank, there are a couple of options open to you. Firstly, the tank will need to be drained and likely removed. If corrosion is minimal, it may be treated with a proprietary fuel tank lining paint. Alternatively, new standard- and large-capacity fuel tanks are available to purchase for a modest cost. If your fuel tank has been repaired in its lifetime with a fibreglass patch repair, now is the time to invest in a replacement tank, as ethanol will soften the resins used, causing the repair to fail. As discussed in the previous chapter, it is not advisable to carry out a welded repair to a fuel tank under any circumstances. Although there are specialists who offer welding repairs to fuel tanks after a very deep cleaning process, the costs involved when compared to that of a replacement tank mean that the latter is the most cost-effective option.

Cork is another material which can be adversely affected by the ethanol content in fuel over time. The only area on a Morris Minor where cork comes into contact with petrol is the fuel tank sender gasket, which at the time of writing is only available as a cork item. Failure of this gasket can result in leakage of fuel into the boot space when the tank is full, as the sender unit is sunk below the highest point of the tank, identifiable by a strong smell of petrol in the cabin after filling up. Solutions to this problem include replacing the gasket with a fresh cork item coated in a fuel-resistant gasket sealant, or making a replacement gasket from scratch – using a cork gasket as a template – from an ethanol-resistant material such as Viton synthetic rubber sheeting.

TIME FOR A TUNE-UP

Having now protected your Morris Minor against fuel leaks, we can move on to improving the engine's state of tune to better suit the new, blended fuel. We should note here that the recommendation from the Federation of British Historic Vehicle Clubs remains to use E5 protection-grade petrol in older cars where possible. This means that although upgrading your fuel system as described above to protect against the ill effects of E10 is a good idea should its use be necessary, altering the state of tune of your Minor should be done to suit the fuel you intend to use most often.

Ignition timing will require adjusting from the BMC-recommended figures (ignition timing (static): 803, 2; 948, 4; 1098, 3° BTDC), although these are a good starting point. Considered opinion is that, starting from these recommended figures, timing should be advanced until 'pinking' – a sound best described as that of a stream of ball bearings being dropped into a baked bean tin – is heard under accelerative load, then retarded until this just disappears.

The chemistry of ethanol dictates that it contains 35 per cent oxygen atoms by weight rather than the pure mixture of hydrogen and carbon found in petrol. The result of this is a leaner burn and the need to enrich the carburettor mixture on your Morris Minor to compensate for this. A Colortune tool is a handy device for correct mixture setting, as is an exhaust gas analyser, whose costs have

Your carburettor's idle mixture will need adjusting to compensate for the leaner-burning fuel.

tumbled in recent years making them well within reach of the home mechanic. Home gas analysers generally measure just CO, which is an excellent indicator of mixture strength. A CO reading of between three and four per cent is desirable. Alternatively, the lift pin at the bottom of the carburettor can be used to raise the dashpot damper slightly with the engine warmed up and idling. Engine speed should increase slightly then fall off when the idle mixture is correctly set.

The mixture may be adjusted on a standard HS- or H-type carburettor by means of the adjuster nut just above the jet. Unscrewing the nut (anti-clockwise) will enrich the mixture by lowering the position of the jet. Tightening the mixture nut (clockwise) will weaken the mixture.

A home gas analyser such as this is handy for setting idle mixture.

3

Access All Areas

Whether it's for day-to-day maintenance or more major work, providing yourself with good access to the area in which you are working is essential for efficient, safe and enjoyable works.

TWO-STAGE BONNET STAY

One of the simplest yet most effective modifications that can be made to the Morris Minor in this regard is the addition of a two-stage bonnet stay. Originally developed by Spares Secretary of the Dorset Branch of the Morris Minor Owners Club, Brian Wood, and now manufactured and sold by ESM Morris Minors, this clever modification makes a superb addition to any Morris Minor at a modest cost.

A straight swap for the original, it directly replicates the action on the original bonnet stay in position one but, with the pulling of a spring pin, allows the bonnet to be raised to a near-vertical position; this is ideal for maintenance and repairs. This position is replicated in the original BMC workshop manual by means of a rope from the bonnet emblem to the rear bumper; however, this has several disadvantages. First, the risk of paint damage on the roof from chafing rope; second, the risk of said rope coming loose and failing at a critical moment; and third, the fact that the rope's route across the boot lid means access to the boot is not possible with it in position. That's not to mention the time taken to set this up and the fiddly nature of removing split and clevis pins from the bonnet stay each time this position is desired.

Speak to any time-served Morris Minor mechanic and they will all have tales of dented skulls or bad backs from leaning beneath the Minor's bonnet. The sprung latch in the centre of the bonnet can be rather unforgiving, as can the sharp corners of the bonnet. These stays prevent all that and also allow a great deal more light into the engine bay, too. The only disadvantage is the recommendation that these should only be raised to the extended position indoors to prevent the risk of wind catching the bonnet outside. They really are a game-changer, though, and once fitted you will wonder what you ever did without one.

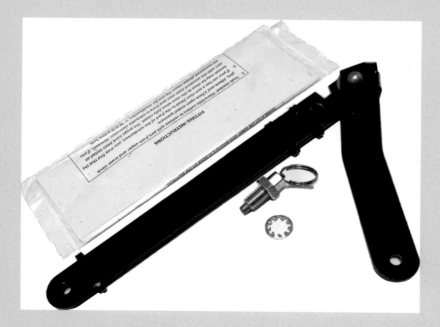

A two-stage bonnet stay is a simple fitment, but one which will save many banged heads.

At the pull of a pin, the bonnet can be raised to an almost vertical position.

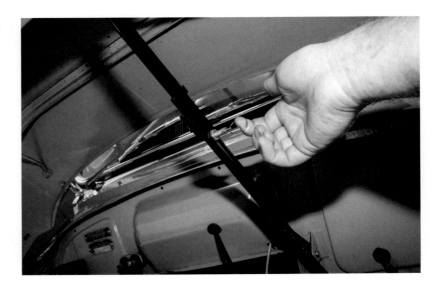

FRONT END REMOVAL

It is possible to remove the engine with the front panels in situ – simply by removing the radiator and turning the engine 90 degrees clockwise during removal with an engine crane. However, if a timing chain requires replacement, an engine crane is unavailable or other major works are to be undertaken in the engine bay, it is the opinion of the author that the modest investment of time to remove the front end panels of the car, along

Front end removal allows superb access to the engine bay.

with the radiator and slam panel as a unit, is well worth-while. This allows for much improved access to the engine, allows the engine and gearbox to be removed as a pair if desired, and allows for easier removal of the engine with or without an engine crane.

The author recalls a flying visit to a French supermarket car park to assist another Morris Minor owner with the removal of their engine this way after a lip seal conversion had failed, resulting in catastrophic oil loss en route to a 'Minors on Tour' club event. On arrival at the car park, the front end of the car had already been removed and two of the party lifted the engine out onto the tarmac. After lunch, the seal had been replaced and the engine could be lifted back in easily for the owner to finish the installation ready to continue their journey.

Here's how it's done:

1) Remove the two nuts that hold the bumper in position. Remove the bumper assembly and set aside.
2) Remove the three 2BA nuts from the back of each 'hockey stick' chrome, which bolt through the front panel to the wings. You may find that the studs come out with the nuts. Remove the hockey sticks and set aside with their fixings.

TIP: Refit fasteners to their original positions immediately after removal to avoid misplacing them.

3) Unbolt the seven 1/4UNF set screws and nuts that hold the bottom of the front panel to the welded front crossmember.

TIP: Use RIVNuts and dome-head allen bolts here on rein-stallation to make for easier disassembly next time.

4) Remove top and bottom radiator hoses. Catch coolant and dispose of it in an environmentally friendly manner. Only save for reuse if it is fresh. Replace with blue ethylene glycol-based IAT antifreeze to the recommended ratio on reassembly.
5) Remove the split pin from the bonnet release rod and lift the rod from its lever.

TIP: DO NOT close the bonnet with the front end still in position until this has been re-fitted.

6) Remove the two 1/4UNF set screws from each side of the top of the slam panel where it meets the inner wings.

7) Carefully remove the front panel, radiator and slam panel as a unit. Set aside carefully.

TIP: On some cars (usually pre-1098) the wiring harness to the N/S headlight and brake light switch is clipped to the bottom of the radiator support/slam panel, as opposed to being clipped to the front cross-member as on later cars. Unhook this to avoid snagging the wiring.

ACCESS FROM WITHIN THE CAR

Lift the carpets in the front of your Morris Minor and you will find a number of brass screws. These allow the removal of two plates, one small, which gives access to the annoyingly situated brake master cylinder (which lives within the driver's side chassis leg), and one large, which allows the gearbox to be removed from within the car.

If the latter is to be achieved, whether for repair, replacement or upgrade either to a stronger ribbed-case Minor or Spridget 'box, or for a 5-speed upgrade, the front seats should first be removed and set aside for safe keeping. Likewise, it is prudent to remove loose carpets and cover others, as things can get very messy very quickly. To remove the carpet from the tunnel cover, and gain better access to the screws, first you will need to remove the gear stick. Unscrew the six self-tapping screws from the rubber draft excluding rubber and lift this out of the way. Then use a $7/16$ socket to unscrew the four set screws that hold the gear stick retaining plate. Carefully withdraw the gear

Master cylinder cover and transmission cover panel screws are made from brass and easily damaged. They are available new, however, and should be replaced if imperfect.

stick and note the anti-rattle plunger and spring mounted horizontally in the remote-change casting. Carefully remove and safely store these to avoid the risk of them dropping into the gearbox. Replace both on reassembly, along with the 'O' ring on the bottom of the gear stick if any are less than perfect.

The countersunk brass screws are easily chewed up by an ill-fitting screwdriver. Be sure to select your weapon carefully, as drilling out and re-tapping damaged screws is tedious and best avoided. If any screws are imperfect after removal, replacements are readily available from the usual suppliers, and replacement is a sensible course of action.

Note the four longer brass screws that thread into the top of the gearbox cross-member. It is important that these are re-fitted in the correct place to prevent the cross-member flexing.

On refitting the cover panel, a bead of sealant should be used to prevent draughts and water ingress. Dum-Dum used to be the preferred choice, but this has not been available for some years now. Body caulking strips, sold for Traveller wood-to-aluminium infill panel strips, are a good alternative. Otherwise, a semi-setting windscreen sealant such as Arbomast can be used here to good effect.

4

Servicing – Do You Really Need to Upgrade?

Before embarking upon any modifications to your Morris Minor, it is important to establish that you are upgrading to provide a genuine advantage over original specification, rather than simply providing a sticking plaster solution to poor performance through lack of proper maintenance, component failure or general wear and tear.

A post-'62 Minor 1000 with its 1098cc engine and 8-inch front drum brakes makes a superb daily driver in standard form, thanks to various upgrades made by the skilled engineers within the British Motor Corporation throughout the Minor's 23 years in production. The author has first-hand experience of this, having used his restored 1969 Minor Traveller in standard form for several long trips, many towing either a small caravan or trailer tent in the UK and Europe.

A recently rebuilt 1098cc engine in standard guise will outperform a worn-out 1275 unit, for example. Having said this, if you are to invest time and money in rebuilding an engine and you are considering upgrading anyway, the investment may be better spent on the larger-capacity engine.

Before going deep, however, it is worth carrying out a thorough service by following the steps below, and keeping your eyes open to potential problems to ensure that you are starting from as good a position as possible. You can then assess how the car drives and decide upon which everyday modifications you may wish to undertake from the following chapters, depending on your intended use and driving style with an open mind.

Use a quality 20W50 grade engine oil to keep your Minor's engine in rude health.

ENGINE

Let's start with the engine, as it is the heart of the car, and an A-series running sweetly really is a joyous thing.

Change the Oil

An oil and filter change should be first on the agenda. Use a good quality 20W50 engine oil, replaced every 3,000 miles or annually, whichever comes first, and use a fresh filter each time.

In standard form, the Minor uses a paper element oil filter. Changing this can be fiddly, and a worthwhile upgrade is the conversion to a spin-on type filter. We will cover this in more detail in a later chapter.

Go for a short run to warm the engine oil and aid drainage. Jack the car and secure on axle stands. Use a ¾-inch AF ring spanner or socket to release the sump plug. Catch the old oil in a drain pan and replace the sump plug with a new copper sealing washer if the old one is less than perfect.

Move the drain pan beneath the oil filter housing and release the long bolt that passes through the oil filter

Original paper element oil filters (left) can be a faff to change. Spin-on conversions (right) will be detailed in a later chapter.

Check and set contact breaker points gap to 0.015in.

Use the 'rule of nine' to set valve clearances.

canister. Support the canister and allow it to empty of oil before removing it. Remove the paper element oil filter and discard, being careful to avoid discarding the stepped washer which supports the element. It often clings to the bottom of the disposable element on a film of oil. Without this washer, the engine will have no oil filtration.

Clean the canister, spring, bolt and washers carefully. Replace the 'O' ring located under the head of the bolt if imperfect. Use a small screwdriver or pick to remove the large 'O' ring from the filter housing still attached to the engine, into which the canister seats. Replace this with the best fitting of the three 'O' rings which will be supplied with your replacement oil filter.

Restack the oil filter assembly with the new element and refit to the engine, lubricating the top of the canister with a smear of clean oil so as not to snag the seal upon tightening.

Refill the engine with oil, remove the low-tension power feed to the coil and crank the engine on the starter until the oil light goes out. Check the filter for leaks and address as required. Reconnect the power to the coil, then start the engine.

Valve Clearances

Next, set the valve clearances. This is important for smooth and powerful running and also ensures longevity for the valve gear. Too small a valve clearance could result in valves not fully closing, reducing compression but also allowing combustion gases to return past the unclosed valve, eroding the closing faces of the valves and seats as well as leaking back into the inlet manifold and carburettor. Too loose, and valves will not open fully, preventing full intake of air/fuel mixture and limiting expulsion of exhaust gases, reducing engine power. Valve clatter will also result from loose gaps, which as well as being an audible racket to contend with from behind the wheel is also an indicator of percussive wear occurring within almost every part of the valve gear. Correct valve clearance for a standard A-series engine is 0.012in when cold.

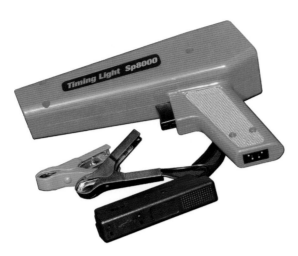

A timing light is useful, though not essential, for setting ignition timing.

Ensure the carburettor dashpot is topped up with the correct oil.

HOW TO SET VALVE CLEARANCES

Use the 'rule of nine' when setting valve clearances on your Minor, i.e. set the clearance on valve number 1 when valve 8 is fully open. Number 1 is the valve closest to the radiator, 8 nearest the bulkhead. Remove the spark plugs to prevent the engine's compression working against you as you turn the engine.

TOP TIP: Mark the HT leads 1–4 (1 being at the waterpump end of the engine) to assist with reassembly later.

Remove the rocker cover, then use your starting handle to turn the engine (or push the car in gear) until the number 8 valve is fully open. Now adjust no.1 valve clearance.

Slacken the adjuster lock nut (either $7/16$ inch AF or ½ inch AF spanner size depending on the rockers fitted to your engine). Slacken the clearance adjuster screw slightly using a well-fitting flat-head screwdriver.

Insert a 0.012in feeler gauge between the rocker and the valve, and tighten the adjuster screw until the feel gauge

slides with just a little resistance between the top of the valve and the bottom of the rocker.

TOP TIP: If you are struggling to achieve quiet valves, this could be a result of worn rockers where the pads act on the valve tops. These are hardened, so will need to be professionally refaced or replaced. As a temporary measure, precise valve clearances can be achieved using a dial test indicator.

With the correct clearance achieved, hold the adjuster screw firmly with your screwdriver and tighten the lock nut before re-checking the gap. Repeat with the other seven valves. Refit the rocker cover. Do not overtighten the rocker cover's fixings.

TOP TIP: The author's preference here is to stick the gasket to the rocker cover with gasket sealant or adhesive, then smear a thin coating of grease on the face which will come into contact with the cylinder head. This will allow for easy fitting as well as removal in the future, and re-use of the gasket as it should come away from the head surface undamaged.

Ignition Checks

Points

The contact breaker points gap should be set to 0.015in (15 thou), and the points should be in good, unburned condition. Burning and pitting of the surface may be an indication of the condenser breaking down. Replace it if in doubt. Also consider the condition of the fibre heel of the points which runs on the distributor's central cam. This wears, particularly if the cam is pitted, and can limit the amount of adjustment available. Cheaper sets of points often use a plastic heel which wears more rapidly than the OE spec fibre. Points and condensers from the Distributor Doctor are widely regarded as the best on the market.

While you are in here, the low-tension wiring should also be checked, as breakdown of the small cable within the distributor is a common, but often missed, cause of breakdown or misfires.

Spark plugs

Spark plugs should be NGK BP6ES or equivalent type from another manufacturer, and should be gapped to 0.025in. The colour and condition of the spark plugs can tell you much about your engine's state of tune. The ideal is a digestive biscuit brown colour, which denotes a good, clean burn of the fuel in the cylinders. Black plugs denote rich mixture. White and pitted plugs denote weak mixture and lean, hot burning which can be damaging to pistons and valves. Oily plugs are cause for concern. Oil burns with a blue-ish hue. Blue smoke from the exhaust under load indicates piston ring and bore wear, time for an overhaul. Blue smoke on the overrun is more likely to be worn valve stems and deteriorated valve stem seals in the head, which are a far simpler fix – but still require the cylinder head to be removed and stripped down. At this point you might consider having the cylinder head converted for unleaded if it has not already been done.

HT leads

HT, or High Tension, leads carry the spark from the distributor cap to the spark plugs. Over time their insulation can break down, leading to arcing (the spark finding an easier path to earth than through the plug) and misfires. Open the bonnet and start the engine in the dark and you may see this spark leakage in action. Old leads should be replaced and oil, dirt and moisture cleaned from leads in otherwise good condition.

Distributor cap

The distributor cap transfers the spark from the coil via the king lead in the centre to the four HT plug leads through the rotor arm (*see* below). Any cracks in the body of the cap, burning or corrosion of the metal contacts or failure of the spring carbon centre bush mean that it is time for replacement.

Rotor arm

The rotor arm distributes the spark to each portion of the cap. Any signs of burning, or loose rivets in non-bonded type arms are a sign that it requires replacement. Red rotor arms from the Distributor Doctor are regarded as the best made and the least likely to fail in service.

Vacuum advance

The vacuum advance unit on the side of the distributor serves to alter the timing under load so that a balance of maximum power and efficiency can be achieved when combined with the mechanical advance of the bob-weights in the distributor. The unit works by means of a diaphragm being acted upon by the vacuum of the carburettor, connected to the distributor baseplate. If this diaphragm is holed, or there is a leak in the pipework to it, this mechanism will not work. A simple test is to remove the vacuum advance pipe from the carburettor end and suck. You should be able to hold a vacuum in the pipe with your tongue. With the distributor cap removed, you should see the baseplate move as vacuum is introduced. If this does not occur, check the pipework carefully for cracking or looseness in its connectors. If all is well here, remove the distributor and suck directly on the vacuum advance unit. If this will still not hold a vacuum, the diaphragm in the unit itself has failed and the unit will require replacement.

Timing

Proper ignition timing is essential for the smooth and efficient running of your Minor's engine. It can be set statically (using a test light), or dynamically (using a strobe). To adjust with a strobe, first disconnect the vacuum advance pipe either from the distributor or carburettor. Connect the sensor wire from the timing light to number one cylinder's HT lead, noting the orientation so that the current is slowing in the direction indicated. Connect the power leads to the battery, taking care that the wires are not likely to be caught up in the fan or other moving parts of the engine. Slacken the distributor clamp so that it may be turned by hand with some resistance. Be cautious of the risk of electric shock while adjusting the distributor position with the engine running – often a sign of insulation breaking down on HT leads or a crack in the distributor cap.

Look for the timing mark on the crankshaft bottom pulley – mark with paint to aid visibility. Note the timing marks on the bottom of the timing cover. Each 'finger' represents five degrees before Top Dead Centre with the longest (left hand when viewed from the front of the engine) representing TDC itself.

Start the engine and raise the idle to 1,200rpm using the idle adjuster screw on the carburettor. Point the timing light at the timing marks and pull the trigger. The light will illuminate every time the spark plug fires. This strobe effect will give the impression of the timing mark on the pulley standing still. In the author's experience, around ten degrees BTDC is ideal when using modern fuel. Rotate the distributor until the timing mark on the pulley lines up with the ten-degree timing mark. Alternatively, most modern timing guns may be adjusted so that the strobe flashes at the desired number of degrees BTDC. In this instance, set the gun to ten degrees and aim to line the timing mark on the pulley up with the TDC marking. This technique makes it possible to re-mark the pulley and cover, having established TDC by means of a DTI gauge through the plug hole, in a more convenient location – particularly useful if the timing cover or front pulley are not of standard fitment. With the ignition timing set, lock off the distributor, reconnect the vacuum advance and lower the idle speed to around 600rpm.

Note: As described previously, this is a great starting point when it comes to adjusting your Minor's ignition timing, however final adjustment should be by trial and error on the road. Advance the timing slightly until 'pinking' is just heard under acceleration, then retard the timing slightly until this just disappears. Therein you will be able to enjoy plenty of smooth power delivery throughout the entire rev range.

Air Filter

An air filter which is clogged with dirt, dust or oil from the breather pipe will reduce the flow of air into the engine, effectively enriching the mixture as well as limiting power. Standard 948 and 1098 air filter elements are cheaply and readily available and should be changed every 3,000 miles (4,828km) or annually, whichever comes first. It is a good idea to at least inspect the condition of the filter before setting the fuel mixture at the carburettor.

Some aftermarket filters can be cleaned, with preparatory cleaning kits from manufacturers such as K&N available for a fraction of the cost of a replacement performance air filter.

Carburettor – Idle Mixture and Speed

If your Minor is in standard form, it's likely that you will find an HS2 SU carburettor bolted to the side of the engine (although early cars feature H2s). However, whether standard or modified, setting up your carburettor properly is essential for smooth and efficient running.

Firstly, establish the profile of the fuel metering needle fitted. A standard 1098 engine should be fitted with an 'AN' needle, and a 948 engine (with HS2 carburettor) an 'M' needle. The taper of the metering needle is what denotes the strength of the air/fuel mixture reaching the cylinders at any given throttle position and under any given load. We will discuss needle profiles for modified engines in Chapter 5.

Although idle mixture can be adjusted by means of the mixture adjustment nut against which the fuelling jet is spring loaded, the mixture up the rev range is predetermined by the thickness of the needle at any given point, as the oil-damped pistons rise and fall with throttle position-induced vacuum. Ensure that the dashpot oil is topped up and that the piston rises and falls smoothly when lifted through the air filter aperture. If it sticks, re-centre the jet.

With this established and with the ignition timing and valve clearances already set, we can turn our attention to the idle mixture. This can be done quite simply by ear. With the idle speed set as desired, the engine warm and the choke off, turn the jet adjusting nut clockwise (unscrewing it and lowering the jet) to enrich the mixture then anti-clockwise to weaken the mixture until the fastest idle speed is achieved. Weaken the mixture (turn the nut anti-clockwise to raise the jet) until the idle speed just starts to fall, then back again until the fast speed is just regained. Finally, reset the idle speed to around 600rpm or as desired.

However, for those with little experience, a more quantitative method may be beneficial. A gunson colortune is a useful device for setting mixture by eye – it is essentially a glass spark plug which can be temporarily fitted in place of one of the standard plugs and allows the user to view the burn colour and, therefore, ascertain the mixture strength.

A yellow flame denotes that the mixture is too rich, whereas a pale blue or white flame denotes a mixture that is too lean. A flame at idle which is a deep-blue colour is ideal. A colour tune is especially useful for tuning twin carburettors (*see* later) as the tool may first be fitted to either cylinder 1 or 2, which are fed by the front carburettor and this adjusted, before being installed in cylinder 3 or 4 and the rear carburettor adjusted.

Another method, now within the realms of the home enthusiast, is the use of an exhaust gas analyser, or CO meter, carbon monoxide concentration being a great indicator of mixture strength. With the engine warm and running at a steady idle, connect the analyser's power cables to your Minor's battery (taking care not to let them become entangled with the fan) and insert the analyser's probe into the exhaust and wait for the reading to settle. Make small adjustments of the mixture nut and allow the gas analyser to stabilise before reading again. Aim for 3–4 per cent CO.

Finally, with the mixture set, re-adjust the idle speed by turning the mixture adjustment screw anti-clockwise to slow, clockwise to increase the idle until a speed of around 600rpm is achieved. The heavier flywheel of a standard 948 engine will tend to allow for a slightly slower idle than the 1098; however, the difference is minimal given the larger diameter of the 1098 flywheel.

If a satisfactorily low idle cannot be achieved by these means, ensure that the adjuster which moderates the lift of the idle with the application of the choke is not over adjusted – i.e. it has a small clearance between it and the cam of the choke mechanism with the choke fully closed. Also ensure that the accelerator cable is not over adjusted. It should have a tiny amount of slack with the throttle fully closed so that the throttle is not being held open by the pedal. There should not be too much slack as to limit the travel of the throttle. Have a friend press the pedal to the floor and ensure that the throttle spindle cannot be turned any further by hand. Ensure that the pedal travel is not being limited by thick or bunched up carpets or underlay.

Health Checks

Having fully serviced the engine, it should now be in fine health. Having established the valve clearances are all correct, now is a good time to perform a compression test.

Remove the low tension lead from the coil, remove all four spark plugs then screw a compression tester into the first plug hole. Hold the throttle open and crank the engine over until the needle settles. Either use the button on the starter solenoid to operate the starter motor or ask an assistant to operate the starter from inside the car.

DANGER: Ensure the car is in neutral before turning the engine over.

Note the reading and repeat for the next three cylinders. Uniform readings are more important than the exact figure reached, but anywhere around 140psi and above is a good reading. Below this could mean either worn piston rings or leaking valves. Pour a little oil down the bores. If the reading improves, the problem is piston rings. If it does not, suspect valves. If two adjacent cylinders show significantly lower compression, suspect a failed head gasket between bores.

GEARBOX

The gearbox should be filled with the same 20W50 specification oil as the engine, and its level checked regularly. It should be filled to the point of overflowing out of the filler plug located on the side of the gearbox. The oil should be checked every 3,000 miles and changed every 24,000 miles for a good quality 20/50. Specialist 20W50 oils

Gearbox tail shaft seal is a relatively simple job to swap.

A lip seal for the gearbox input shaft is well worth considering.

designed for use in classic Minis that share oil between the engine and gearbox are worth considering. Whichever oil you choose, ensure that it is of GL4 specification to avoid damage being caused to the yellow metals in the gearbox. More information on specialist oils can be found at www. classic-oils.net.

Look out for leaks from the gearbox and address them as necessary. The most common points of leakage are from the tailshaft seal at the rear of the 'box where the propshaft enters and the front input shaft seal within the bellhousing. The former is a relatively straightforward fix, necessitating the draining of the oil, removal of the propshaft and drifting off of the old tailshaft seal before the replacement can be carefully tapped into place. The latter is a little more complex, necessitating gearbox removal to access it.

A leak at the front of the gearbox will often result in a slipping clutch. This should not be mistaken, however, for a leak from the back of the engine, from the crank's scroll seal. A common cause for this leaking is incorrect breathing of the engine and excess crankcase pressure, which is something we will examine later in this book. A lip seal conversion for the front plate is available. It is a worthwhile upgrade, as a fix for a leak or even if the engine or gearbox are removed for another reason, given the amount of time and effort that stripdown to access the seal takes.

CLUTCH

A heavy clutch on a Morris Minor is a common complaint and it can easily be assumed that a hydraulic clutch upgrade (*see* later) is required to resolve this. However, in standard form, with an OE spec pressure plate (rather than heavier diaphragm plates which may be fitted to prevent slipping with a more powerful engine), the clutch feel should be light and controllable.

The problem of a heavy clutch is often down to wear in the cross-shaft bushes either in the gearbox or the chassis. These are available to purchase individually or as a kit, and it is the author's experience that, more often than not, wear in the bush is combined with wear in the holes in the linkage too, so it is worth the modest investment to purchase a kit of parts and replace the lot.

Note that the clutch adjuster rod is a common point of failure. It can wear through and snap, so keeping the one that you take off in the boot as a spare is a very good idea.

A complete clutch linkage and bush kit will not break the bank and will transform pedal feel over worn originals.

That brings us nicely on to the point of adjustment. A maladjusted clutch will be difficult to use. If the pedal is set too low, it may be tricky to engage gears as the clutch is not fully disengaged. Similarly, if the clutch is set too high, the clutch may not fully engage, causing clutch slip as well as premature wear both on the friction plate and carbon release bearing.

Adjustment may be carried out by means of the two nuts on the clutch link rod. First, the locknut must be slackened then the main adjuster nut can be turned so that the pedal has the recommended amount of free play (1.25in for 1098/0.75in for 948).

Ensure, while you are there, that the clutch return spring is present and in good condition. If this breaks, the pedal will rest at the point of engagement, which can rapidly wear the carbon release bearing.

DIFFERENTIAL

The differential, or final drive, serves both to change the direction of drive from the propshaft to the wheels, but also to allow the outermost wheel on a corner to travel further than the innermost wheel. It is an important part of the car's drivetrain, but maintenance here is often ignored. As with the gearbox, oil should be checked every

Quality oil is the key to a long service life.

3,000 miles and changed every 24,000 miles, and replaced with EP90 gear oil to GL4 specification.

Leaks on the rear axle can often be traced to a blocked breather, which allows excess pressure to build up in the axle casing, forcing oil to breach the weakest seal, be that hub or differential pinion. Located on top of the axle casing, the breather consists of a plastic tube and a cap. To clear the breather, simply pop off the cap and run a pipe cleaner or even a piece of wire through the tube, ensuring the two cross-drilled holes in the tube are clear, before replacing the cap.

The final drive should be quiet in operation. A differential which howls will require specialist intervention and it is often more cost effective to simply replace the unit for a known good item. If a change is required, then this is a good opportunity to consider upgrading to a different ratio – we will cover this in detail in Chapter 7.

BRAKES

Well set-up drum brakes, especially the later 8-inch items fitted to Minors from the 1962 model year and easily retrospectively fitted to earlier cars, can work very well indeed. It is tempting to consider a conversion to disc brakes as the only option to make a Morris Minor stop well, but that does not have to be the case. Yes, disc brakes have myriad advantages, including improved cooling (especially useful if you drive your Minor hard); however, as with all of the modifications we will cover later in this book, it is worth experiencing the brakes in fully functioning standard form before using an upgrade as a sticking plaster solution.

With the road wheels removed, slacken the brake shoe adjuster cams and remove the drums, tackling this process a corner at a time. Note that brake dust can be harmful and care should be taken here. Inspect the area around the cylinders for fluid leaks (that cylinder will require replacement if any leaks are present) and clean away dust with soapy water or a preparatory brake cleaning spray.

Grip each piston in turn and attempt to move them within their bores. You may need to draw down the brake shoes that sit upon them using a screwdriver as a lever. If the pistons do not move freely, they may be seized and require replacement. Further analyse this with the brake shoes removed.

Check that all of the brake shoes have plenty of friction material left, and that the drums' working surfaces are not badly scored, glazed or pitted. Once thoroughly cleaned of brake dust, lightly damaged surfaces may be dressed with coarse sandpaper.

Adjust brakes until they lock, then back one click.

If the above checks are in good order, refit the drums and adjust so that the brakes lock, then back one click so that light dragging of the shoes on the drums can be felt.

On the front, there are two adjusters per drum. These should each be adjusted in turn to achieve even dragging from each. On the rear, there is just one adjuster; however, care should be taken to ensure that the handbrake is off (and its lever on the rear of the brake backplate in the fully off position) and the cylinder is free to slide in the backplate before adjustment is made. Apply the brakes a couple of times and re-check adjustment, as this may settle the shoes.

When inspecting the rear brakes, also check for evidence of oil leaks from the axle into the drum, which will need rectifying as a matter of urgency. Contaminated shoes must be replaced.

With the brakes fully adjusted at the drums, apply the foot brake and assess the free-play in the pedal. If excessive, it may be adjusted by means of the push rod between the pedal and master cylinder. This can be accessed by removing the carpet in the driver's footwell and unscrewing the master cylinder access plate.

Conventional (DOT 4) brake fluid should be changed every three years, as it is hygroscopic in nature, which means that it attracts moisture from the air. This water content can cause corrosion to the cylinders as well as causing the fluid to become more compressible than it is designed to be. We will discuss upgrading to silicone fluid in Chapter 9.

SUSPENSION

Regular maintenance of the suspension on a Morris Minor is essential to avoid failure. Top and bottom trunnions on the front uprights should be greased at least every 1,000 miles, with the wheels raised from the floor.

Note: If grease is not pushed from the dust seals, it likely is not entering the trunnion correctly. It will pay to remove the afflicted trunnion, clean and inspect the threads, replace the grease nipple and reassemble with replacement parts as required. Failure of a trunnion on the road is extremely dangerous.

Check bushes for wear. Rubber bushes in particular can deteriorate quickly. If you spot signs of wear and tear, it

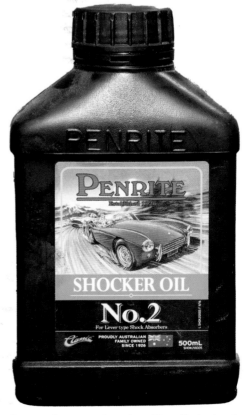

Ensure lever arm dampers are topped up with quality shocker oil.

makes sense to replace at least a full axle set of bushes. It is also worth considering upgrading to polyurethane. We will discuss the options and show you how to do this in Chapter 11.

Although there is not much to be adjusted on a Morris Minor's suspension geometry, taking your car for a four-wheel alignment check can tell you much about its condition, and whether it is repair or upgrades that are required to improve its driving characteristics.

Tracking can be simply adjusted (specified toe in is $\frac{3}{32}$ in or 2.5mm) and camber may be adjusted by means of shim washers added behind the torsion bar eye bolts. A 3mm washer should add approximately one degree of negative camber.

Serious differences in camber and caster from side to side may indicate poor welded repairs, misaligned chassis legs, bent or incorrectly fitted components, all of which must be identified and rectified before opting to upgrade.

ELECTRICS

Looking after the health of your electrical system is vital to ensure that everything works as it should. For example, dim lights may be down to poor connections or corroded earthing points, and simple cleaning may be enough to improve functionality enough to render an upgrade unnecessary. Even so, if any electrical upgrades are to be effective, it is imperative that the car's electrical system is in rude health.

Restoring proper function to a poor connection is quick and easy. The Minor employs bullet-type Lucar connectors throughout its original harness. First, work the connector back and forth in its holder. Often this abrasion is sufficient to clean loose corrosion from the surface and restore function. If not, the connector should be split apart and cleaned with abrasive paper and/or a preparatory electrical contact cleaner spray. Take note of any wires that are frayed or corroded where they enter the male side of the bullet terminal, often presenting as green/grey deposits. In this case, it is worthwhile swapping the bullet terminal for a new one, first cutting back the wire slightly and stripping off the insulation to reveal sound, uncorroded, cable. These brass connectors can be either crimped or soldered in place, or both. If they are to be crimped, it pays to invest in the correct crimping tool (Autosparks part number AST23). If they are to be soldered, either as an alternative or in addition to crimping, once again strip back the insulation to reveal clean cable, then dip the exposed strands in flux paste. Feed through the connector and crimp if desired, then apply heat and feed the solder into the end of the terminal. The flux will help the solder flow where it needs to go.

For the female side of the connectors, cleanliness is key. Replacement connectors are readily available and having a good stock in your arsenal is always a good idea, if they cannot be cleaned effectively by abrasion/contact cleaner. Around the car, there are female connectors screwed directly to the body, which provide an earth. These are the most common causes of electrical faults and must be clean and corrosion free, as must be their securing screws. It is worthwhile here working the

Check all terminals are correctly and firmly fitted and for corrosion, which will cause high resistance.

screws back and forth a little, as well as ensuring that the holes they are screwing into are free from paint, which can act as an insulator.

Battery connections should also be clean and free from corrosion, as should the main earth points both directly from the battery and from the engine/gearbox to the car's body. Poor earthing to the engine is often to blame for poor starting, and can be checked by connecting a jump lead directly between the battery earth and the engine (perhaps a clean head stud, of course first ensuring that the lead will not become entangled in the fan assembly at the front of the engine). If starting is immediately improved, ensure that the engine to body earth strap is present and its connections are clean. Also remember that the starter motor itself earths through its securing bolts between the engine backplate and the gearbox bellhousing. If both of these are covered in a thick layer of paint, then the starter will not be receiving a good earth.

The main live feed from the battery to the starter solenoid then from the solenoid to the starter is just as important as the engine earth in ensuring reliable starting. Ensure they are both in good condition and the terminals are free from corrosion. Also note any breakdown in the insulation of these heavy cables and replace them if they are less than perfect. Pre-made cables of the correct length are available cheaply enough from the usual suppliers.

One final note: when reassembling any of these connections, it is a good idea to allow them a little protection from future corrosion. Petroleum jelly is often used on terminals to prevent corrosion and, in the author's experience, works well. It is also inexpensive and readily available.

STRUCTURE

Another important note is that there is no point bolting modifications to a car, or even judging a need for them, if your Minor is not a sound basis to begin with. Rot may allow body flex, as well as prevent secure location of key suspension components. Similarly, if your Minor has been poorly repaired in the past, key mounting points may not

be in the correct location, resulting in alarming handling characteristics. If you are concerned that this may be the case, a diagram of key body dimensions may be found in the BMC workshop manual, from which a jig may be constructed if required.

Such is the ubiquity of the Morris Minor, almost every rot spot is catered for by a range of repair panels. If you are not confident tackling the repairs yourself, there are many experienced specialists who will be able to take on the job for you. It is very uncommon for a Minor to be rotten beyond saving; however, the costs involved may outweigh the value of the car in some cases, if welding work is to be outsourced.

Check your Minor's underside condition carefully. Almost nothing is irreparable, however you must start from a sound basis before embarking on any modifications.

Part II: Modifying the Morris Minor

It might appear that we have digressed in the previous chapters from this book's main subject matter; however, it is incredibly important to approach any modifications with a clear understanding of the car's capabilities in standard form.

Modifications should be seen as improvements over this standard form, taking more modern developments to make the Minor a better car on today's roads. They should not be used as sticking plaster solutions to disrepair and lack of proper servicing.

Clearly, if you are considering modifications on a project, rather than on an already operational car, it will not be economical to rebuild it to standard guise only to pull it back apart immediately to modify it. In this case, carefully consider your requirements and perhaps even speak to local owners and enthusiasts about the possibility of riding as a passenger in or, with correct insurance in place and the permission of the owner, driving a selection of both standard and modified Minors to get a feel for exactly what you want to achieve with your own project.

5

Engines

Yes, that's right, it's what you have been waiting for. If you have bought this book, you are probably looking to get more power from your Minor, and this is the section in which we will explore that possibility. Not yet, though. First, we will talk a little about the engine's ancillaries and a variety of sensible modifications that can be made here. These can be considered whatever size A-series engine you have fitted to your Minor – and whether standard or increased levels of power output are desired.

ENGINE ANCILLARIES

Spin-on Oil Filter

As mentioned in Chapter 4, the original canister type oil filter is a fiddly thing to replace, often leaks and, if installed incorrectly (i.e. the washer beneath the filter is misplaced, as so often happens), will not filter the oil at all, leading to premature engine wear, expense and misery.

If you are maintaining your Morris Minor yourself, a spin-on filter will speed up the process and keep mess to a minimum. If you entrust servicing to a third party, the foolproof nature of a spin-on filter change, which requires no specialist knowledge, will give you peace of mind that the job will have been done correctly.

A spin-on oil filter conversion, then, really does make sense – and it is a modest investment. At the time of writing, a conversion kit including replacement mounting studs, cast housing, nuts, spring washers and a filter can be purchased from ESM Morris Minors for just £22.50, as well as being available from a number of other suppliers.

Converting to spin-on is straightforward, and is best done to coincide with a planned oil change. Undo the oil feed pipe to the filter, remove the two retaining nuts that secure the original housing to the block, remove the 'blocked filter' warning light wire, if fitted, and loop in insulating tape out of harm's way and remove the original housing from the block. Remove the male-to-male pipe fitting from the original housing and fit it to the new casting.

Tighten the two nuts that you have just removed against each other on each stud, and use a spanner on the innermost nut to wind the long mounting studs out of the block. Replace these studs with the shorter studs in the conversion kit in the same way, noting the coarse ($^5/_{16}$ UNC) thread screws into the block. Smear the supplied gasket with a little sealant, then slide it along the studs

A spin-on oil filter is a worthwhile upgrade to simplify servicing.

the filter into place on the underside of the new casting. Tighten by hand only.

A three-legged filter removal tool that fits on a ratchet is a worthwhile investment to aid removal come oil change time.

Magnetic Sump Plug

While on the subject of oil, another simple and worthwhile modification is the addition of a magnetic sump plug. Again, this is something worth fitting during a planned oil change as part of a service, but for less than £10 including a new washer, a magnetic sump plug will attract any magnetic debris shed by your engine into one place, out of harm's way, at the bottom of the sump. Not only will this prevent metallic particulates from being drawn into the oil pump, but it will also give you a good indication of engine wear when it is removed and cleaned at the next service.

Electronic Ignition

Although there is nothing inherently 'wrong' with the Minor's original points and condenser ignition set-up, regular adjustment is required to keep the points' gap correctly set (15 thou) as the 'heel' wears as it runs on the distributor's central cam. Also, some modern replacement contact breaker points and condensers are cheaply produced and prone to failure. Be wary of purchasing cheap condensers, as they have been known to fail after a short period of use, or even not work at all straight out of the

A magnetic sump plug will help to keep magnetic fragments away from the oil pump, as well as serve as an indication of engine wear.

and against the block. Ensure the oil feed drilling is not blocked and is fully encompassed by the gasket. Slide the cast filter housing along the studs until it abuts the gasket, then secure with nuts and spring washers. Do not over-tighten this, as the housings can crack.

Refit the oil feed pipe to the male-to-male fitting in the filter housing, then fill the new filter with fresh engine oil to speed up the priming process, smear the filter's integral rubber 'O' ring with fresh oil and screw

Remove the points, condenser and low tension lead. Keep these safe, along with the condenser screw.

Apply heat paste to the bottom of the electronic module and fit in place of points.

Magnetic trigger ring slips over distributor cam.

Re-fit rotor arm and secure wiring.

box. Yellow wire condensers, as sold by the Distributor Doctor and supplied via a number of Morris Minor specialist parts suppliers, are of much higher quality and tend to last well, in the author's experience. Contact breaker points originally used fibre heels. These lasted far better than the plastic heels used on many cheap reproduction sets. Again, those sold by the Distributor Doctor are of OE specification and tend to last well.

If, however, you want to move away from points and condensers, as manufacturers have done with modern cars, a good, cost-effective upgrade is to replace the points and condenser set-up for an in-distributor electronic ignition module.

Such electronic ignition modules may be purchased to be fitted into your existing distributor, or pre-fitted to brand new units. The module in the accompanying images is from Accuspark, but its fitting procedure and function are similar to modules from other sellers. It is possible to fit the electronic module in situ, but it may be easier to remove the distributor to carry out this conversion, noting its position before removal for replacement in the same place – although note that the ignition timing will need to be reset once the module is fitted.

Note the polarity of your Minor before purchasing your electronic ignition kit. Most are designed for negative earth application, however positive earth variants are available. See Chapter 12 for direction on converting your Minor to negative earth.

First the points, condenser and low-tension lead should be removed from the distributor baseplate. The electronic ignition kit will come with a small packet of white paste. This is a silicone heat sink paste which must be applied on the underside of the module baseplate to prevent it overheating in use. The module can now be fitted to the distributor base plate in place of the points and condenser. A magnetic ring will also be supplied in the kit. This should be fitted over the distributor's central cam to trigger a spark.

The module is fed by two wired feeds, which will need tying away from the distributor's moving parts with a small cable tie. The rotor arm can be refitted, and the distributor reinstalled (if it has been removed) to the engine and the cap replaced. The red wire should be wired to the positive side of the coil, the black wire to the negative side of the coil. Ignition timing should then be adjusted. Note that precise static timing is not possible with electronic ignitions and so a strobe should be used as described in Chapter 4.

Note: Although electronic ignition modules are generally reliable, like anything else they can fail. It is sensible to slip the points, condenser, low-tension lead and condenser securing screw into a zip-top bag and stash them in the boot or glove box so, should the electronic ignition module fail, it can be swapped for the original points and condenser set-up at the roadside to get you going again.

Duplex Timing Chain Conversion

The timing chain connects the camshaft to the crankshaft via a large and small sprocket, allowing the crankshaft to turn four times for every revolution of the camshaft. The OE specification timing chain fitted to the Morris Minor's A-series engine is a 'Simplex' single chain item, which can quickly stretch and become slack, resulting in inaccurate cam timing and noisy running as the slack chain rattles and in extreme cases contacts the side of the timing case.

To combat this problem, 'Duplex' (double chain) upgrades are commonplace and an incredibly worthwhile upgrade if ever the timing chain needs intervention. Kits, which include a pair of pulleys with two rows of sprocket teeth, a new duplex chain, gasket, oil seals, lock washers and two countersunk allen head screws (required to replace the two ¼ UNF set screws positioned behind the crank pulley to allow clearance for

Timing of a standard duplex timing chain should be set 'dot-to-dot'.

Note that the lower two front plate mounting setscrews require replacing with countersunk allen-headed screws.

Crankshaft oil thrower must be refitted with its 'F' marking facing forward.

the deeper sprockets) are available from Morris Minor parts specialists for less than £30 at the time of writing. Fitting the kit is relatively straightforward, with access the biggest challenge. As such, it makes sense to check the condition of the timing chain and replace if necessary if the engine is removed or the car's front panel

removed for whatever reason. It is possible to undertake this conversion with just the radiator removed for access; however, a 90-degree drill angle drive (or angled drill) will be required in this case to countersink the holes in the front plate for the new allen head set screws to be installed.

HOW TO FIT A DUPLEX TIMING CHAIN

1) Gain access to the timing chain cover either by removing the front panels of the car (*see* Chapter 3) or removing the radiator (*see* note on access above).

2) Disconnect the battery to avoid accidentally engaging the starter motor while working on the engine, then slacken the dynamo/alternator tension and remove the fan belt.

3) Unfold the crankshaft nut tab washer, remove the 15/16AF bolt/starter dog then withdraw the front pulley from the engine. This may be tricky as the engine will likely turn before the thread stiction is broken. Lock the car in gear and ask an assistant to apply the brake. Alternatively, use an impact wrench and solder to shock the bolt loose.

4) Remove the set screws that attach the timing chain cover to the engine front plate, These are a mixture of lengths (the two shortest are at the bottom to allow clearance for the sump to be removed without fouling on protruding threads) and diameters (¼ and 5/16 UNF). Note their positions for reassembly.

5) Remove the front cover, being prepared for a small amount of oil leakage as the gasket seal is broken. Remove traces of the old gasket from both surfaces.

6) Knock back the camshaft tab washer and use the same 15/16 in AF socket to remove the camshaft gear retaining nut.

7) Temporarily refit the crank nut/starter dog and turn the engine so that the dots on the timing gears match up. This will aid reassembly.

8) Use a puller or pair of levers to gently draw both crank and cam sprockets from their respective shafts, and discard both sprockets and chain.

9) Behind the crankshaft sprocket, you will find two ¼ UNF front plate fixing set screws. The hex head on these fixings will foul on the thicker duplex sprocket, so these must be removed and replaced with a pair of ¼ UNF countersunk allen screws (supplied as part of the conversion kit). If you have not removed the front panels from the car, this is where things get tricky. An angled drill or adapter must be used with a correct bit to countersink these two holes

in the front plate. If the front of the car is off, or the engine is on the bench, this is much more straightforward. Take care to clean all swarf from the front of the engine and fit the new screws using threadlock, as they no longer benefit from the shakeproof washers that were originally fitted.

10) Loop the new duplex timing chain over both new duplex sprockets in much the same way that the originals were removed, aligning the timing marks. Locate the crankshaft sprocket first, on its keyway, then the camshaft sprocket. You may need to rock the engine on the lower sprocket to allow the camshaft keyway to engage. Check again that the timing marks are lined up and adjust the sprocket's position in the chain if necessary before easing both sprockets all the way 'home'.

11) Replace the camshaft securing nut with a fresh tab washer and tighten fully before bending the tab washer so it prevents the nut from working loose. Fit the crankshaft oil thrower with the 'F' marking facing forward.

12) Replace the lip seal in the timing chain cover if it is less than perfect. Again, a replacement should be supplied in the kit.

13) Refit the timing cover with a fresh gasket and your choice of gasket sealant. Secure loosely with two fixing bolts, then align the bottom seal by temporarily fitting the front pulley with grease or oil on its working face. Nip up the two loose bolts, then remove the pulley and re-fit the remaining timing cover bolts. Tighten diametrically to 6lb ft (¼ UNF) and 14lb ft (5/16 UNF).

14) Refit the front pulley with a fresh tab washer, tighten the bolt/starter dog to 70lb ft.

Note: Riveted front pulleys can fail. While it's off, check rivets for tightness and the pressed steel elements for cracking or deterioration. Replace if imperfect and consider fitting a harmonically dampened front pulley, as fitted to later A-series engines.

15) Refit the fan belt, radiator and front end panels (if removed). Start the engine and inspect carefully for oil leaks.

Precision Timing

They say the secret to comedy is timing: the same applies to getting the most out of your engine. For the engine to run efficiently, the inlet and exhaust valves must open at exactly the time the camshaft designer intended in relation to the position of the pistons in the bores. Although standard 'dot to dot' timing is sufficient for most road engines, once performance becomes the aim of the game, it is worth investing in ensuring that the cam timing is spot on. 'Rotaslide' or 'Vernier' timing gear conversions are a great option here, allowing quick and easy adjustment of cam timing during the engine build. Although precision timing can be carried out by means of offset woodruff keys in the crank end (Minispares offer keys offset between one and nine degrees), a Vernier adjustable gear gives far greater precision and can be adjusted in situ without the need to strip down and reset between each measurement. Setting the camshaft timing with a Vernier timing chain is a specialist task, and one which we do not have space to explain in intricate detail here. What follows gives an overview of the process. For more detail, and guidance on timing an engine before the cylinder head is fitted, visit www.calverst.com, where an excellent instructional article can be found under 'technical info'.

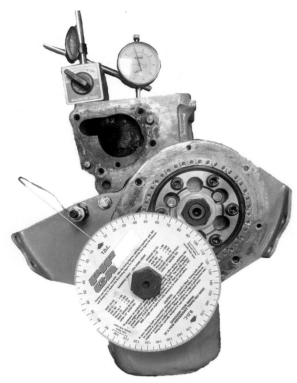

Vernier timing chains require careful setting up.

Setting Vernier timing

Initially the Vernier timing set should be fitted in much the way as the duplex set described previously up to step 10. Once the assembly has been initially fitted, the cam timing can be checked and adjusted as required.

With the timing chain and sprockets fitted 'dot to dot' as previously described, a 360-degree protractor should be fitted to the front of the crankshaft and retained by the front pulley bolt or starter dog. Using a dial test indicator through number 1 cylinder's plug hole, the crankshaft should be rotated so that cylinders 1 and 4 are at top dead centre. A pointer, mounted to the engine, can now be set to correspond with the zero degrees marking on the crankshaft protractor.

Re-position the DTI on top of the inlet valve on cylinder 1 (second in from the front). Rotate the crankshaft forward until maximum lift is achieved and the needle settles at the bottom of the valve's movement (when it is fully open), then zero the DTI. Rotate the crankshaft backwards until a reading of 0.025in is observed, then forward gently until a reading of 0.010in is achieved. Note the reading shown by the pointer on the protractor.

Repeat in the opposite direction, turning the crankshaft forward until a lift of 0.025in is achieved, then back until the DTI needle reaches 0.010in. Note the degrees shown here. Add the two figures together and divide the answer by two. The resulting number is the number of degrees relative to TDC at which the inlet valve is fully open.

Compare this figure against the camshaft manufacturer's specified angle and adjust, if necessary, by slackening the allen screws that hold the cam sprocket to its central hub, then rotate the crankshaft fore or aft as required, before locking off the allen screws and repeating the measuring process until the correct cam angle is achieved.

Note that it is possible to set the cam timing with the cylinder head removed, by measuring lift on top of the pushrod. This is ideal if the engine is still in build; however, Mini tuning specialist Keith Calver observes, on his website, that the calculated figure will be two to three degrees retarded from the figure measured at the valve and, therefore, this must be taken into account.

Carburation

If you want a little more power from your existing engine, this can easily be achieved by allowing more air/fuel mixture in and out of the combustion chambers through the

An HIF38 SU carburettor here is mounted to a 1.5-inch cast combined inlet/exhaust.

The HS4 carburettor pictured was originally fitted to a 1275 Morris Marina, but is a good upgrade for both 948 and 1098cc Minors.

An HIF44 Carburettor is a good upgrade for 1275 engines, with a BDL needle.

addition of a larger carburettor (or even a pair of carburettors) and a better-flowing exhaust system.

Although a variety of carburettor types have been fitted to Morris Minors over the years, including Webers for out-and-out performance gains, we will focus here on the various SU carburettor upgrades most commonly fitted to the side of the Minor's A-series engine. The SU carburettor is a simple fuel metering unit which can offer a good balance of usable power and economy when correctly set up.

Understanding SU carburettors

The HS2 carburettor is the most ubiquitous Morris Minor carburettor, developed by SU in 1958 as a replacement for the earlier H2 carburettors. The 'HS2' nomenclature stands for **H**orizontal (the plane in which air flows through the carburettor) **S**eparate/**S**ide (Separate/Side mounted float bowl with a flexible jet feed), with **2** denoting a throttle aperture two eighths of an inch over one inch (1.25 inch measured from the throttle disc side). Similarly an HS4 car- burettor is four eighths of an inch over one inch (1.5 inch) and the HS6 has a 1.75-inch throttle disc. Series MM Minors used an H1 (1 inch and ⅛ th with solid mounted float).

Developed in 1972, HIF-series carburettors (Horizontal Integral Float) initially used the same imperial numera- tion as their HS forebears (HIF4/HIF6 replacing HS4 and

HS6); however, this was soon changed to adopt the metric system with the introduction of the HIF 38 (38mm = 1.5 inches – i.e. HIF38 is the same inlet throat diameter as the HS4 carburettor) and HIF44 (equivalent to the HS6).

If looking to fit SU carburettors from elsewhere in the BMC/BL range to your Minor, a useful addition to your bookshelf will be a spare parts and specification catalogue from the SU carburettor company. This excellent publica- tion includes reference tables that include OE specifica- tions and applications for every SU carburettor ever avail- able. It will come in very handy for both identification of potential purchases, as well as for tuning. Jet and needle combinations are clearly outlined and, as a starting point, it pays to ascertain the nearest OE application to your own set-up at least as a baseline before having your Minor set up on a rolling road. These catalogues can be obtained

Twin carburettors offer good power advantages but can be tricky to set up.

through www.sucarb.co.uk. Alternatively, the site also offers a useful online carburettor needle comparison and analysis spreadsheet. Carburettor rebuild kits as well as a full array of needles and jets are available to purchase through the same website.

What are the options?

From standard, all but the earliest Minors were fitted with an HS2 carburettor, with a 1¼ inch inlet; however, owners often upgrade to larger SU carburettors from elsewhere in the BMC/BL model range.

One step up from standard, and a common fitment to both 1098- and 948-engined cars, is the HS4 carburettor or its more modern HIF38 counterpart. Just a quarter of an inch larger in diameter than the standard HS2, the difference that this carburettor can make to performance is quite remarkable, especially when teamed with a larger diameter exhaust.

A single outlet cast inlet/exhaust manifold from a Morris Marina may be used here in place of the original Minor manifold to allow the fitment of the larger carburettor and 1.5-inch exhaust using a suitable conversion downpipe (ESM part number EX123). Alternatively, if the standard 1¼ inch exhaust is to be retained, for that distinctive Minor 'Parp', the original manifold may be sawn in half, so that the inlet is removed. Aftermarket aluminium inlet manifolds, often with provision for water pre-heating, are readily available from a range of suppliers including Minispares (www.minispares.com). The final option is to combine an aluminium inlet manifold with a three-branch tubular exhaust manifold feeding a 1.5-inch system. We will be discussing exhaust options in more detail later in this chapter.

Twin HS2s are also a common fitment, and were fitted as standard to the 948cc Frogeye Sprite and later the 1098- and 1275-powered MG Midget and later model Sprites. These offer a fine improvement in fuelling; however, they are trickier than a single carburettor to set up, requiring careful balancing.

An HS6 or HIF44 carburettor is a great pairing with a 1275 engine, and can be fitted via an aftermarket cast aluminium manifold to provide reliable power. This is the largest diameter carburettor it is recommended to fit to an A-series engine, and was fitted to BMC's sporting models such as the MG 1300 from standard.

Twin HS2, HS4 or HIF 38 carburettors are also options on the larger capacity A-series, but the same caveat as before applies, in that they can be tricky to set up and the performance gains are marginal. The author recommends a single HIF44 carburettor as the best pairing with a 1275 engine.

Carburettors gave way to single- (SPI) then multi- (MPI) point injection as time marched on, with these ECU-controlled systems able to achieve greater efficiency than the analogue carburettor. It is possible to use the SPI set-up from a late Mini on a Minor, or aftermarket kits such as those from www.specialist-components.co.uk; however, this is not a common upgrade.

Setting up your new carburettor

Idle mixture can simply be set either by adjustment of the mixture idle nut (H- and HS-type carburettors) or the idle mixture screw (HIF-type carburettors) in the manner described in Chapter 4.

Mixture strength across the rev range, however, is predetermined by the taper of the carburettor's needle, which must be removed and swapped for an alternative or reprofiled by an experienced tuner. The SU Carburettor Company's website (www.sucarb.co.uk) offers information on needle specifications as well as general tuning information. Similarly, www.mintylamb.co.uk/suneedle is a great resource, offering the opportunity to graphically compare needle profiles.

There is no magic bullet in terms of needle choice, as engine specifications, compression ratios and wear, exhausts and back pressure vary wildly from car to car, meaning that there is no 'one-size fits all' approach. For best results it is highly recommended that you have your car set up on a rolling road; however, a good starting point can be achieved by studying the OE specification for other cars within the BMC/BL range that best match your Minor's set-up. The chart on page 45 offers a guide to this for most common carburettor fitments.

A wide band Lambda sensor may be fitted to the exhaust manifold and wired to a display in the cabin used to display the live mixture data to the driver. This is particularly useful during set-up and tuning, as well as a trial-and-error approach to carburettor selection. It should be noted that a lean mixture, particularly at periods of high load, can be damaging to the engine due to the high burn temperature. The display of this Lambda data, then, is useful to alert the driver to potential problems before any damage is done. This should not be necessary once the car has been properly set up on a rolling road, although it may be useful as an early warning system should your carburettor or inlet manifold develop an air leak and run lean, for example.

Engine	Carburretor(s)	Needle(s)	OE Fitment	Recommended Exhaust
948cc	HS4 or HIF38	ADH	Mini 1000	Standard 1.25 or 1.5inch
948	Twin HS2	V3	Austin Healey Sprite MKII	Standard 1.25 or 1.5inch
1098	HS4 or HIF38	ABP	Mini 1100	1.5 inch
1098	Twin HS2	AN	MG Midget MKII	1.5 inch
1275	HS4 or HIF38	DZ	Austin 1300	1.5 or 1.75 inch
1275	HS6 or HIF44	BDL	MG 1300	1.5 or 1.75 inch
1275	Twin HS2	M	Mini Cooper S	1.5 or 1.75 inch
1275	Twin HS4 or HIF38	ADP	Metro 1300	1.5 or 1.75 inch

Forced Induction

Superchargers and turbochargers have both been fitted to Morris Minors with good effect. However, careful consideration needs first to be given to whether the engine, and the rest of the drivetrain, will be up to handling the additional strain that forced induction will impose upon them. A lower compression ratio is required, as are stronger pistons that will not be melted by the higher temperatures involved in a blown engine, with dished, forged Omega pistons a popular choice.

The A-series was turbocharged from the factory in the MG Metro Turbo, and so the camshaft, pistons, turbo and manifolds from one of these extraordinary hot hatches are a good place to start. However, when it comes to period supercharger conversions, the choice is limited to the aftermarket, with Shorrock having been the go-to for many years.

Another Cowley product, however, offers a 21st-century solution for supercharged A-series. The Eaton M45, as fitted to the Mk1 BMW MINI Cooper S, has become a popular fitment on classic Minis and, therefore, conversion parts are available to make fitting this more modern blower onto the side of an A-series reasonably straightforward. VMAXCART, based in Surrey, UK, offer a range of supercharger kits for A-series engines, as well as offering individual components including a specially machined bottom pulley for anyone wishing to piece a conversion together from component parts rather than purchase a complete kit. More information, parts and prices can be found at www.vmaxcart.com.

Exhausts

It is all very well getting more air/fuel mixture into the engine with improved carburation, forced induction or even injec-

The author's own supercharged Morris Minor uses an Eaton M45 'blower' from a BMW MINI Cooper S.

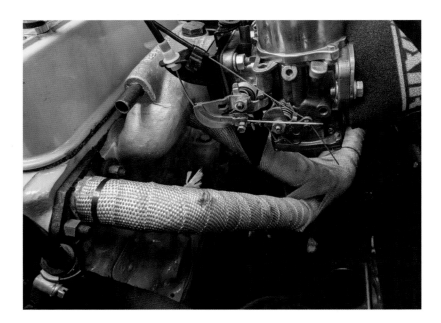

Note the heat wrap on this three-into-one LCB tubular exhaust manifold, which helps to keep under-bonnet temperatures down.

tion (as fitted to very late Minis and available as kits to purchase to convert your earlier A-series if desired); however, in order to see any real power increase from such modifications, the exhaust needs to be able to expel these additional gases, too – within reason. Of particular importance on naturally aspirated engines is back pressure. Too much back pressure from the exhaust restricts flow, but too little and the flow of exhaust gases will be detrimentally slow: imagine the effect of putting your finger over the end of a hose pipe; too much restriction and you will limit flow; too little, and the water will dribble out with high volume but very low pressure. Find the point of compromise and you will have both a rapid flow and high volume of water leaving the end of

the hose. The rapid flow has the effect of drawing combustion gases out of the engine, improving performance. For a forced induction system, imagine a pressure washer – the pump (supercharger or turbocharger) – pushes the water through the end of the hose at both a higher volume and pressure than can be achieved by an open hose.

At the front of the exhaust system is the manifold, which takes exhaust gases from the cylinder head's three ports (cylinders 2 and 3 have internally siamesed ports, with gases leaving the head casting through a single, central port) to the main exhaust system.

Standard Minors use a 1¼-inch cast manifold, which combines inlet and exhaust in one component. The

Interim downpipe EX123 is fitted here between the 1.5-inch cast inlet/exhaust manifold and large-bore exhaust on the author's convertible Minor.

A stainless steel exhaust system is a fit-and-forget item, whereas mild steel systems are prone to corrosion.

Morris Marina uses a similar system, but enlarged to 1½ inch inlet and exhaust, offering the ability to add an HS4 or HIF38 SU carburettor alongside a larger diameter downpipe and exhaust. Downpipes designed to fit between this manifold and the range of 1½-inch exhaust systems available off the shelf are available – ESM part number EX123.

Tubular exhaust manifolds offer improved flow compared to cast items and can be more simply used in conjunction with cast aluminium aftermarket inlet manifolds allowing a greater choice of carburation. Long Centre Branch (LCB) manifolds compensate for the siamesed port by means of an increased volume in the centre tube to reduce the back pressure caused by it receiving sets of combustion gases for every full combustion cycle of the engine. 1½-inch ID LCB manifolds are readily available from Morris Minor specialists, and even larger (1⅝-inch ID) manifolds are available to order from manufacturers such as Maniflow.

Behind the manifold, big bore exhaust systems are available off the shelf both in 1½ inch (most commonly used and available from Morris Minor specialists) and 1⅝ inch (less common and only beneficial for forced induction cars or highly modified 1275 engines), from exhaust specialists such as Maniflow (www.maniflow.co.uk). Exhaust fitting kits for the above systems are available from the same suppliers.

THE IMPORTANCE OF BREATHING PROPERLY

Even the best and freshest engine build will leak oil if it is not breathing correctly. Breathing refers to the relief of excess pressure from the engine crankcase. Too much crankcase pressure will result in oil leaks, which can range from annoying to catastrophic. Although almost all A-series engines leak to some extent, a drip is acceptable, a torrent is not.

Factory breathing methods changed throughout the A-series' lifespan and a little trial and error may be required depending on your particular engine as, in the author's experience, there is no 'one-size fits all' solution.

Rocker covers fitted with breather take-offs should be connected to the negative pressure outlet of either the carburettor or air filter, depending on your set-up, and should be fitted with non-vented caps. Vented oil filler caps, which should be fitted to non-breathed rocker covers, allow air to be drawn into the top of the engine from the atmosphere. This is beneficial if the flow is required from the top of the engine down through the crankcase and out through canister breathers to negative pressure either via the tappet or timing chest breathers. If, however, the rocker cover breather is plumbed to negative

pressure, a breathed cap will simply allow air to be drawn through the cap, then out of the breather, negating the usefulness of either device.

Both 948 and 1098 engines feature removable tappet chest covers, which incorporate breathers. Some use canister breathers, which should be plumbed to the carburettor negative pressure, others feed direct to the ground. In the case of the latter, a breathed rocker cover is recommended.

The 1275 engine tends to be the trickiest to breathe correctly. Under no circumstances should the timing cover breather be blanked off completely, as this will always lead to severe breathing problems and oil leaks. If a 1275 engine is fitted and the original mechanical fan retained, the canister must be sliced in half vertically and a plate welded to the front to make it a D profile to allow the fan to clear. Alternatively, MED Engineering (www.med-engineering.co.uk) offers a rather fetching billet aluminium timing cover that uses an angled adaptor in place of the canister – an elegant bolt-on solution.

Canister-type breathers, whether fitted to the tappet chest or timing cover, incorporate a steel gauze that can become blocked over time and prevent proper breathing. This must be cleaned out either by soaking in degreaser or by removing the gauze completely. If the former option is chosen, ensure that the gauze is fully dry and the canister empty of any fluid before refitting to the engine.

The author has observed that the commonly successful breathing set-up on the majority of A-series engines uses a non-breathed rocker cover oil filler cap, with a breather pipe from the rocker cover into a T-piece, with a pipe to the carburettor's negative pressure take-off from the second T outlet and a third pipe from either a timing cover or tappet chest breather into the T.

Excessive crankcase pressure may be relieved by means of an additional breather on the boss for a mechanical fuel pump, if machined in your block, however this should not be necessary if the engine is in good order and investigation should be carried out to find what is causing this excessive pressure.

Cylinder Heads

During the A-series engine's near 50-year lifespan, it underwent many changes and was used under the bonnet of a great variety of cars, from its humble beginnings in the 1951 Austin A30 to its swansong in the final Rover Minis of 2000. Cylinder heads were one of the many developed components and changing or upgrading them can bring huge benefit to your Minor, especially when teamed with improved carburation and a nicely flowing exhaust.

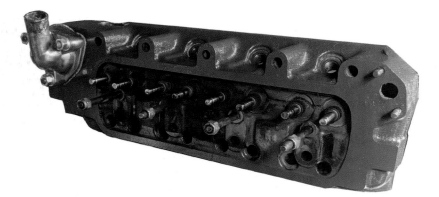

The 12G940 cylinder head, as fitted to most 1275 engines, can be fitted to the Minor's 1098, but the block may require 'pocketing' to prevent valves hitting the machined surface.

Later 'top hat'-style valve stem oil seals are a worthwhile upgrade over the Minor's original 'O' rings.

vs 26.1cc) from standard. The larger chamber is better shaped for clean and efficient combustion; however, the increased capacity must be taken into account when calculating the engine's compression ratio and the head skimmed as required. It is worth measuring the chamber volume of the cylinder head, however, before undertaking any machining work, as it is likely that the head will have been skimmed previously, either to alter its compression ratio or to restore flatness to a warped surface.

The 12G940 cylinder head found on most 1275 A-series may also be fitted to smaller capacity engines; however; the larger valves will sit outside of the smaller engine's cylinder bore, and will require the block to be machined (pocketed) to allow clearance and prevent the valves contacting the block surface – particularly at high RPM.

For 1275 engines, the original 12G940 casting works well out of the box, and carburation will likely remain the limiting factor on most road-going, naturally-aspirated engines. It is possible, however, for larger than standard valves to be fitted to this cylinder head if desired.

Whichever cylinder head you choose to use, it is worth considering whether it has been converted (or was factory-fitted) to use hardened valve seats for use with unleaded petrol. Factory fitted 'heads were fitted with unleaded seats from 1989; however, fitting unleaded seats to an earlier head is a bread-and-butter task for most good machine shops.

Valve guides should be checked for excessive wear (remove valve, invert it and insert into the top of the guide to check for play) and replaced while the 'head is at the machine shop. Fresh valves at this point are recommended, too. Valves working up and down in guides inevitably draw some oil down the valve stem as they work; however, this should be mitigated through use of quality valve stem seals (blue smoke on the overrun denotes worn guides/deteriorated seals). 'Top hat' type seals, as fitted to late-model cylinder heads are best, and although only

Casting numbers can be found on the top of the cylinder head beneath the rocker cover, adjacent to the valves. What follows is a basic overview of the most common cylinder head swaps; however, other publications have covered this subject in far more detail and are well worth a read, especially if high power output is desired.

For 1098 and tuned 948 engines, the 12G295 cylinder head is highly prized. Featuring larger inlet valves than the standard 1098 12G202 head (1.214in as opposed to 1.151in) with a larger combustion chamber (28.3cc strictly required on the inlet valves (as the suction of the inlet stroke works to draw oil from the rocker area through the valve guide and into the cylinder), there is little harm in fitting a set of eight, one on each valve.

While the cylinder head is apart, consider fitting a set of double valve springs. These consist of a smaller spring inside of the main spring. The two different diameter springs have different resonant frequencies, so as well as applying more force to the valve cap, snapping the valve shut quicker and more effectively than the standard set-up, they prevent valve bounce by never both reaching their resonant frequency at the same time.

Some performance engines use eleven, rather than the original nine, cylinder head securing studs. Machining for this is a specialist job; however, it is beneficial if out and out power is desired, and is certainly a good sign that money has been spent on an engine if these additional studs have been added. Similarly, porting and polishing the cylinder head to improve flow and combustion area over what is possible from the factory-fresh rough casting is highly beneficial, but is a job best left to a specialist. Tackling this task at home if you are inexperienced more often renders a 'head scrap than results in any genuine improvement in power output.

Rocker Gear

Standard rocker ratio is 1.28:1 and both pressed steel and cast, sintered rockers were fitted to the A-series engine from the factory over its long lifespan.

Roller-tipped rockers of 1.3 and 1.5 ratio are available for the A-series engine. These reduce the side loadings on the valve, pushing it straight down the guide, reducing wear and also offering quieter running. The higher ratio valve offers more lift, depending on the camshaft used. Performance tuning specialists such as MED Engineering or Calver ST offer a range of high-quality roller rockers and are able to offer advice on the best components for your build and intended use.

IDENTIFYING A-SERIES ENGINES

Before embarking on any sort of modification or engine swap, it is important to be sure what engine is already fitted to your Minor. Although identification by year of production should be fairly straightforward, do not take it for granted that the original engine, or even the original capacity engine, is fitted in your car.

This section should also be helpful in identifying a potential donor engine, and understanding the key differences that may require further work to allow retrofitting to your Minor. It is unlikely that you will be removing the whole running gear from an MG Midget to fit to your Minor, for example – you are more likely to be blowing away the cobwebs from a long-dormant lump under a workbench or in the middle of a rainy autojumble, which may have sat unused for many years and its lineage be unknown. However, it is simple enough to tell the various inline A-series engines apart by inspecting their casting features.

Roller-tipped rockers are a worthwhile, if expensive, upgrade, particularly to a performance-orientated engine build.

803 A-series features non-remote oil filter below the dynamo. Image taken from LCV brochure, courtesy of Richard O'Brien

Note '950' cast into 948 cylinder block below removable tappet chest covers.

An 803cc A-series engine, as fitted to early Series 2 Minors, features an oil filter mounting cast into the block just beneath where the dynamo mounts, low down on the distributor side of the engine. Removable tappet chest covers also feature on the opposite side of the engine

which, along with the different position of the non-remote filter, help to differentiate this early A-series from its 1275 Marina/Ital counterparts which we will describe later. Both 948 and 1098 engines, and the 1275 fitted to the MG Midget, feature remote oil filters.

The 948 engine is most easily identifiable by the number '950' cast into the side of the block, just behind the front plate on the opposite side of the block to the distributor and dipstick. Like the 803, this casting features removable tappet chest covers.

The 1098cc engine was originally fitted with an aluminium tag with the numbers '1098' pressed into it in the same location as the 948's cast ID; however, this is often lost if the engine has been cleaned in an acid bath or simply served a hard life. The rule of thumb in this case is that if it does not have an oil filter casting above the distributor (803), and does not have 950 cast into the block (948), but it *does* have removable tappet chest covers, then it is a 1098cc engine.

The 1098 engine was also fitted to the MG Midget, but with some changes. For the sportier MG, it featured larger (2-inch) main bearings (the Minor received 1.75-inch mains) for strength, as did the 1275 units fitted to Midgets, Marinas and the A+ fitted to Itals. Note that the sumps are not interchangeable for this reason.

There are three types of inline 1275cc engines that you may come across. We will start with the most similar to the Minor's own 1098cc unit – the 1275 fitted to the MG Midget. This is a visually very similar block to the 1098 item, but with 1275 pressed into the aluminium identity tag rather than 1098. Its oil filter is in the same place as

1098 A-series also features removable tappet chest covers.

1275 Midget engine is the only 1275 A-series with a remote oil filter.

1275 Marina engine. Note the position of non-remote oil filter, above the distributor.

1275 A+ features strengthening ribs on its block.

Note that the A+ engine uses a different distributor drive (left) to its earlier counterparts.

the 1098 engine, bolted to the side low down on the block forward of the distributor. There are no removable tappet chest covers on any 1275 engine, as they compromised the block's strength and so were deleted.

The Morris Marina was fitted with another development of the A-series from its launch in April 1971. Featuring an oil filter take-off upside down above the distributor, the Marina block is identifiable from its A+ successor by smooth block sides. The otherwise very similar A+ block that was introduced in 1980 with the Morris Ital features a lattice of strengthening ribs on its sides, which aided torsional rigidity.

Aside from these visual differences, there are myriad internal changes that were made through the engine's development, including variation in distributor and camshaft drives, big end journal diameters, crankshaft bolt patterns and so on; however, once you have established which engine you have, sourcing the correct parts to fit it should be reasonably straightforward.

ENGINE UPGRADES WITHIN THE A-SERIES FAMILY

948 to 1098

As discussed, the 1098cc engine fitted to late Minors is perfectly suited to daily use. It also responds well to bolt-on modifications such as carburettors and exhausts, which serve to take performance to the next level without breaking the bank.

If a 1098 engine is to be fitted to an earlier car, it is recommended that it is paired with a 1098 (or 1275) ribbed-case gearbox, which offers improved strength over the smooth-case 948 unit.

If this is not viable, however, it is possible to mate a 1098 engine to a 948 gearbox if this is the desired option. To do this, the pressed steel backplate, heavy flywheel and small diameter clutch from the 948cc engine must be used.

Note that the 948 gearbox uses a different clutch fork and release bearing to the 1098 gearbox to make up for the difference in pressure plate offset between the two engine set-ups, so this must also be retained.

1098 to 1275

The 'ultimate' A-series upgrade has to be the 1275cc unit taken either from an MG Midget or from a Morris Marina or Ital.

The Midget engine is the most straightforward swap, and best resembles the Minor's original unit. The MG Midget utilises the same ribcase gearbox casing as the 1098 Minor with slightly stronger internals, so the Midget's original backplate can be used. The Midget's engine mounts in much the same way as the Minor, so the original MG frontplate can be used, too.

At the rear, however, things get trickier. 1275 MG Midget crankshafts use a six-stud bolt pattern with offset dowels to locate the flywheel. Although re-drilled 1098cc flywheels are available from the usual specialists, they are suitable only for use with Marina/Ital crankshafts, where the dowels are not offset. One solution is to have a 1098 flywheel re-drilled especially to Midget stud pattern by your local machine shop, or to use the original MG Midget clutch with a hydraulic conversion, or modified clutch linkage to compensate for this additional clamping force of the Midget pressure plate. However, the author has experience of successfully utilising an off the shelf flywheel re-drilled for the non-offset Marina/Ital crank and removing the one offset dowel from the end of the Midget's crank.

Note the six-stud bolt pattern and offset second stud (bottom) on the MG Midget crankshaft.

ESM Morris Minors can supply a re-drilled Minor flywheel to suit the Marina's stud pattern. Note equally spaced locating stud holes.

The stronger clamping force that the Midget clutch benefits from is only really required when the 1275 is in a high state of tune and, regardless, alternative pressure plates are available to increase clamping force on the original Minor clutch. (*See* Chapter 6).

Marina and Ital 1275 engines require a little more work to fit, although nothing beyond the reach of anyone contemplating an engine swap. You will require a few items from the standard Minor 1098 engine, so it is worth holding on to the engine you remove as a donor until the conversion is complete.

Starting at the back, the Marina's flywheel should be ditched; however, a standard four-stud Minor flywheel will need re-drilling by a specialist machine shop in order to mate with the five-stud pattern on the end of the crank. Luckily, help is at hand, as a number of Minor parts suppliers sell re-drilled flywheels for this application on an exchange basis (ESM part number 10M001SCK).

Although not essential, it is always a good idea to have the entire crank assembly including flywheel and clutch dynamically balanced together, especially if mixing and matching components that were not balanced together during factory assembly. This not only allows smoother running and higher revving, but also increases the life of the engine's main bearings, as unwanted centrifugal loads are removed. If you are unwilling or unable to remove the crankshaft assembly from your engine, or if a rebuild is not on the cards, balancing specialists

Vibration Free in Bicester, Oxfordshire, can help. They are able to balance the assembly in a built engine by mounting the short block, inverted, on a specialist machine, removing the sump then rotating the engine via a belt on the flywheel.

Moving forward through the engine, the Marina's backplate will need swapping for a Minor item while the flywheel is removed, and re-sealing with a new gasket. The block itself can be used unmodified, but do remove the engine mounting brackets and rubbers, if still present, from the side of the casting. The front plate will need swapping for a Minor (or Midget) item that incorporates mounting points for the original Minor engine mounts. Consider upgrading to a duplex timing chain at this point, too, as the timing gear will require removal from the engine to swap the front plate.

All 1300 engines are fitted, from standard, with a canister breather on the front timing cover. It is essential that this is retained to prevent oil leaks; however, if the original fan is to be retained (it is far simpler and otherwise beneficial; to fit an electric fan to avoid this problem – *see* Chapter 12), it must be cut in half vertically and a flat plate welded on its front to form a 'D' profile to allow the fan to clear. Alternatively, MED engineering can supply a beautifully engineered CNC-milled aluminium timing cover which uses a smaller angled take-off in place of the original catch can.

ENGINE BUILDING BASICS

Although we are not going into detail about building engines in this book (there is a raft of information and opinion available elsewhere on the subject), it makes sense to mention a few engine building basics in this chapter.

As we have mentioned previously, a well-built 1098cc A-series will outperform a tired 1275, and a tweaked 948 can be a joyous thing indeed. So whether you intend on rebuilding a larger capacity engine for fitment into your Morris Minor, or whether you are simply set on recapturing the horses your Moggie left the factory with, following a few simple principles will help to ensure success.

First and foremost, cleanliness is key. From the point of stripdown through to the first start-up, keeping the inner workings of your engine spotless should be the utmost priority. And while we are on the subject of stripdown, equip yourself with a number of boxes, bags, an indelible marker pen and handful of luggage labels, blue roll, clean rags, brake and clutch cleaner, degreaser, scrapers and razor blades and a good supply of disposable gloves to help you on your way. A small bench-top parts cleaner is also a good investment for a modest outlay and having compressed air and a blow-gun on hand will be a great help when it comes time for reassembly. Cling film is a cheap and effective way of keeping large components dust-free and is also ideal for wrapping the completed engine for storage until the time comes for it to be fitted into the car.

WHAT ABOUT MINI ENGINES?

Although more readily available, transversely mounted front-wheel drive A-series from the likes of Minis, Maestros, ADO16s, etc., are not straightforward swaps and are best avoided unless a complete scratch build is desired and a complete undamaged inline starting point cannot be found.

Although the bare castings are the same, 12G1279 being the casting numbers for both transverse Mini and inline Midget pre-A+ 1275 blocks, there are several key differences in their post-casting machining that present engineering challenges when it comes to converting a Mini-style inline engine for rear-wheel drive applications. Additional dowels and threaded mounting holes must be added in the rear of the block to accept the backplate and gearbox for rear-wheel drive application, which would never have been required for transverse applications where the gearbox is positioned in the sump of the engine. Threads need to be cut into the oil pick-up to accept the Midget-type oil pick-up (no longer available new), as well as additional ¼ UNF sump mounting threaded holes.

Additionally, machining will be required in the rear of the engine block to accept a scroll seal or alternatively upgrade to a lip-type oil seal.

Similarly, A+ Mini engine blocks may be converted for use with rear-wheel drive; however, additional consideration must be given to the requirement for an alternative distributor to suit the later casting.

Conversion is a major machining job and a replacement crankshaft and sump will also be required from a donor inline 1275cc engine to complete the build. (Note that 1275 bearing caps, as well as those fitted to 1098 Midget engines, are larger in diameter than smaller capacity blocks and therefore a standard Minor sump will not fit one of these engines. Similarly, crankshafts are 1275 specific.) Specialists are able to convert Mini transverse engine blocks for rear-wheel drive applications, however the costs involved in this are significant.

Transverse A-series such as those from Minis are best avoided.

TOOLING UP

There are not many specialist tools required to strip and rebuild an A-series engine; however, a decent set of AF sockets and spanners, a torque wrench, a good selection of screwdrivers, feeler gauges, plastigauge and ideally a deep 15/16 in AF socket for the starter dog and camshaft nut should enable most tasks to be undertaken with relative ease. A small copper/hide hammer and a parallel punch set will be useful, too. A dial test indicator (DTI) and crankshaft protractor will make checking/setting valve timing possible if you want to go further than timing 'dot-to-dot' and an engine stand which allows the engine to be rotated 360 degrees with ease makes the job a whole lot easier and safer. Engine stands are available cheaply enough brand new and most can be easily deconstructed for storage; however, as a tool which may be used once and never again, they are often available second hand for very little outlay. Alternatively ask at your local car club to see if anyone has one you can borrow for the duration of your engine build; you won't regret it.

Abnormal damage and scoring such as that displayed on these camshaft bearings begs the question 'why?'. Careful investigation is essential.

Stripdown

Organisation is key when stripping the engine, and so a selection of various-sized zip-lock bags, boxes, indelible markers and luggage labels are critical to avoid confusion come reassembly. It is also worth noting that this is not the time to throw anything away – you may need to refer back to the old, worn parts later for specification. Take plenty of photographs throughout the disassembly process and keep matched components (such as pushrods and cam followers) organised to allow them to be re-paired if they are reused when the engine is reassembled. Inspect all parts carefully on disassembly for wear and note issues as you find them. It is easy to forget or overlook issues found during disassembly until the time comes to put the engine back together and you find you are missing something critical.

Crankshaft journals should be checked carefully for wear, and may be re-ground by a machine shop to accept thicker bearings to compensate for the material removed. Allow the machine shop to assess, measure and grind the crankshaft and take their advice on the finished dimension before ordering replacement bearings. Lightly worn crankshafts may simply require a polish. Bearing tolerances can be found in the general data section of your workshop manual. Cylinder bores should also be inspected for wear, with a distinct step in the top of the bore not uncommon after high mileages. Again, a machine shop will be able to measure, re-bore and hone the cylinders to suit an oversize set of pistons.

Cam bearings, too, should be checked and replaced if necessary while the engine is with the machinist, as this is a specialist task to get right.

Cleaning

Cleanliness is the most important factor in any engine rebuild, and it is important to note that parts returning from a machine shop that may have been washed in a parts cleaner are not ready to fit. Their machine shop clean is merely a starting point, and all oil ways, drillings and both internal and external surfaces should be cleaned meticulously with a preparatory cleaner and degreaser before being blown through with an airline. Brake and clutch cleaner is a good final stage in the cleaning process. Water ways, too, should be completely clean and clear – the rear of the block, around cylinder four, is a common spot for corrosion to build up.

> **TIP:** The author advocates sending bare cylinder blocks to be chemically dipped before they are sent to the machine shop, in order to clean corrosion from water and oil ways of rust, scale, paint and oil residue.

Component choice

As with most things, buying the best you can afford is the best way to ensure that an engine you build for your Minor will serve you well into the future.

At the most basic level, consideration should be given to the quality and age of the fasteners used throughout

Having been hot alkali-dipped at Lenton Treatments in Leicester, this 1275 Midget block looks as good as the day it was cast.

the build. For the want of a nail, after all, a shoe was lost, and consequently, so the proverb goes, so was the horse, the battle and the kingdom. Poor quality flat or spring washers have the ability to compress when tightened or under vibrations in use. Spring washers that expand and escape from their seating not only have the potential to allow the tightness of that fixing to be compromised, but also may find themselves in the inner workings of the engine, ready to cause carnage. Similarly, anyone who has enjoyed the pleasures of removing a snapped cylinder head stud from a block (typically the last one to be tightened, and just flush with the top of the block) will guard against re-using aged studs which have been stretched, corroded, bent, and otherwise ruined by the ravages of time. Similarly, cheap nuts whose threads pull out just as the specified torque figure is reached are no fun at all. Quality undamaged used or new fixings, then, are the way to go. American-made ARP fasteners (www.arp-bolts.com) are the gold standard, and promise to allow accurate and consistent load to be applied to them without stretching, or compression of washers, and come supplied with assembly lubricant to ensure that stiction between nut and thread does not introduce error into the torque figure.

Similarly, pistons, bearings, camshafts, pushrods and followers all vary massively in both price and quality. Consider your application and budget before selecting components and do not be afraid to re-use old components so long as they are unworn and spotlessly clean. A good used set of pushrods, for example, will likely outlast a cheap reproduction set which may be of inferior quality.

Oil pumps are the heart of your engine, pumping vital lubricant to where it is needed most. Do not skimp here – always replace an oil pump with a quality item. No matter what the price point of the pump you select, however, it is important to check the clearance between the impeller and the housing against your manual. This is because it is commonplace to find excessive clearance here, especially in cheaper pumps, which could lead to poor oil pressure and a dramatically shortened engine service life.

Balancing

One of the most effective ways of extracting additional power from your engine as well as improving its life expectancy is to have both the rotating and reciprocating components within the engine properly balanced.

Just as a wobble from an imbalanced wheel can cause a significant wobble through the steering wheel, so any

A bench-top parts washer is a good investment, as is an air compressor with blow gun for cleaning oil ways.

imbalance in the rapidly rotating crankshaft assembly can set up a significant amount of vibration within the engine, exerting huge forces upon its bearings. Simple maths tells us that a small vibration at low RPM will be magnified by the square rule as engine revolutions increase – so for every doubling of engine revolutions, the force from the imbalance is quadrupled.

Oil gallery plugs should be drilled out to allow the oil ways to be cleaned properly before a rebuild. It is a good idea to drill and tap the plug holes to accept screw-in plugs which allow for easier cleaning in the future.

Plastigauge is useful for a final check of bearing clearance.

Crankshaft end float is best measured with a Dial Test Indicator, but can be checked using feeler gauges.

Steve Smith, Managing Director of Vibration Free Engineering (www.vibrationfree.co.uk), explains:

'Vibration is wasted energy. A well-balanced engine will not waste energy through vibration, and unwanted side loadings on main and big end bearings will be significantly reduced, resulting in a longer service life. A well-balanced engine is far smoother, too, making for a far more pleasant driving experience.'

Machining and Tolerances

Never take anything for granted. It is not unknown for incorrectly-sized main or big end bearings to be supplied with re-ground crankshafts, pistons to be supplied with wrongly-sized ring sets or for machine shops to simply get things wrong. Rarely are these problems insurmountable if discovered early by due diligence in the pre-assembly stage, but any one issue could become a major obstacle to success if left unchecked.

It is highly recommended to check bearing clearances with Plastigauge during assembly. Although this is not the most precise engineering measuring

tool, Plastigauge is a useful way of double-checking bearing tolerances. A small piece of Plastigauge is broken off and inserted on a crankshaft journal before a bearing cap is installed and tightened to its specified torque. The bearing cap is then removed and the spread of the Plastigauge checked against a chart

Use an inverted piston to centralise piston rings when checking clearances.

supplied with the Plastigauge pack, which equates to an approximate clearance. A working clearance of 0.5 thousandths of an inch is specified for main and big end bearings. Anything outside of this requires further investigation.

Piston ring gaps should be checked by sliding the bare rings down their respective bores, centring using a piston with another ring installed on it. The gap can then be checked with feeler gauges, against the specified gap given by the piston manufacturer (aftermarket pistons) or in the workshop manual.

Re-assembly, care and attention

Care and attention at every stage should be observed, with cleanliness a key driver of success. It is worth keeping a roll of clingfilm in your workspace and wrapping the engine and any cleaned components between work sessions. It is also a good idea to keep a straight edge handy to check all gasket surfaces for flatness. Rocker, timing and tappet chest covers, front and back plates as well as the more obvious cylinder head and block surfaces, are not uncommonly warped and must be flattened before assembly.

Quality gaskets and sealants should be used throughout, and all fixings torqued correctly. Ensure all threads are cleaned before torquing to ensure an accurate reading. Keep your workshop manual handy as a guide to torque specifications and working clearances.

Always rotate the crankshaft two full revolutions after fully tightening any big end or main journal, to ensure that no tight spots present themselves. If the crankshaft locks after one bearing is tightened, investigate. An 'it'll be fine' approach rarely is.

Running In

When starting the engine for the first time, care must be taken to establish that the engine has sufficient oil pressure. Remove the spark plugs and disconnect the fuel pump. Turn the engine on the starter until the oil light goes out or, better still, oil pressure of around 60psi is achieved on an oil pressure gauge. If your car is not fitted with an oil pressure gauge and you do not wish to fit one (more on this in Chapter 14), an engineer's gauge is a worthwhile investment and can be screwed into the block in place of the oil pressure switch.

Once oil pressure is established, check thoroughly beneath the engine for signs of oil leaks and rectify as

Warped surfaces will never seal. Use a straight edge to check.

Quality fasteners such as these ARP cylinder head studs and nuts which ensure a consistent torque is reached and maintained are a sound investment on a high-end engine build.

required. Check the oil level and top up as necessary. The spark plugs may be replaced and a first start attempted. If a replacement camshaft and followers have been fitted, it may require 'bedding in' – follow your camshaft manufacturer's instructions.

Once out on the road, excessive revs should be avoided for the first 500 miles or so, as should labouring the car in too high a gear at low speed. Oil should be changed after the first 100 miles, then again after 500 miles before the normal recommended 3,000-mile interval can be observed. Note that a magnetic sump plug as previously described is highly recommended for a new engine to keep metallic swarf away from the oil pump and, by extension, the crank and camshaft bearings, as well as being a great visual aid for the amount of wear in your engine come change-time.

MODERN ENGINES AND MORRIS MINORS

Although the A-series engine family can be upgraded to suit modern motoring, with power and reliability upgrades aplenty possible, there are also those who choose to go down the route of more modern engines in their Minors. When considering swapping to a more modern power plant, your attention should be drawn to Chapter 1 and the definition of a vehicle of historic interest. Consideration should also be given to the rest of the drivetrain, not necessarily capable of taking the power, and power delivery, of a more modern engine without modification or replacement.

The Fiat Twin Cam engine was a popular choice for many years, but as scrapyards emptied of crusty Fiats and the availability of spare parts dwindled, those running these impressive engines today tend to do so more for nostalgia of the modifying scenes of old rather than any real 21st-century benefits.

Ford's Zetec engine is a common choice nowadays. However, fitment of this superb modern engine does require some significant modification to the Minor's structural bulkhead. This is a well-trodden path, though, and individual owners and specialists alike – including JLH Morris Minors, who successfully campaigned a Zetec-powered racing Minor for many years and who are able to supply many parts necessary to carry out this conversion in your own Minor – have worked to create a recipe for success which should be easy to follow or adapt for anyone considering this conversion. It is well worth following advice from someone who has already carried out this conversion before attempting it yourself – there is little point in attempting to reinvent the wheel.

An interesting development in recent years, in the same 'scrapyard spirit' as Fiat Twin Cam swaps of old, is the development of a kit to fit the Nissan CG engine to A-Series-powered classics. Barratt Engineering in the south of England have developed a bolt-in conversion for this descendant of the A-series to be fitted to the MG Midget and, at the time of going to press, were in the process of developing a similar kit for the Morris Minor. More details will be found at www.barrattengineering.co.uk once the kits are in production.

Myriad other engines – including V8s, V6s, K-series and others – have all propelled fast road Minors over the years, and it is likely that engines still on the drawing board today will eventually sit in place of an A-series under the bonnet of a Morris Minor somewhere.

Ford's Zetec engine is a popular modification for those seeking 21st-century performance and reliability. However, the conversion is a mammoth undertaking.

6

Gearboxes

Upgrading the power of your Minor is just a small cog in the overall search for usability. A good gearbox and final drive (next chapter) is essential for transmitting that power to the wheels. However, power upgrades are not the only reason to consider gearbox upgrades.

The post-'62, ribbed case Morris Minor gearbox is the strongest factory version fitted to the Minor and, therefore, the easiest to use without crunching between gears (note that first gear is not equipped with synchromesh on any inline A-series gearbox). A five-speed gearbox even behind a standard engine is a great upgrade to balance acceleration with a reasonable cruising speed, without needing to compromise either by altering final drive ratios.

Availability may also play a part in your decision. Reconditioned gearboxes are an expensive option, but the value of second-hand 'boxes remains reasonably low. If, for example, your 948cc Minor's gearbox is on its last legs, and a known good 1098 gearbox can be found for a reasonable price, the simplicity and relatively inexpensive process of upgrading rather than seeking to replace like-for-like may well be desirable. MG Midget gearboxes are well supported in terms of new parts availability; however, core units are hard to find and are relatively expensive.

803 GEARBOX

As with the 803cc engine, it is unlikely that you will be looking to retain the relatively weak original 803 'box if any kind of upgrades are intended. However, thanks to the wonderfully antiquated 'pudding stirrer' gear stick in Series 2 Minors, which enters the cabin much further forward than the 1000's stick, it is worthy of note.

This charming feature of the Series 2 is something that would be lost with the simplest gearbox swap option, of simply replacing the bolt-in transmission cover panel with a later one and fitting a 948 or 1098-derived gearbox. (Note, it may be necessary to replace the chromed handbrake lever for a later painted type in this instance, too).

Having said that, it is possible to retro-fit the 803's non-remote change with its distinctive gear stick position and feel to a 948 'box. In simple terms, the tail casting of the 803 gearbox replaces the gearbox extension housing,

803 gearbox is identifiable by the position of the gearstick.

which incorporates a remote change on the later gearbox. This 'best of both' approach allows the 948 gearbox, with its much improved ratios, to be fitted without upsetting the charming interior aesthetic of these early cars.

A similar conversion is possible with the 1098 'box; however, some modification is required to the reverse selector rod. If this is a conversion you are interested in undertaking, more detailed information can be found at www.mirabelleclassiccars.co.uk.

948 GEARBOX

The 'smooth case' gearbox fitted to 948 cars can be perfectly fine for a standard car when in good condition, but it does suffer from weak synchromesh – in particular on second gear. This necessitates a slightly steadier driving style with a pronounced pause when changing into second gear. It is rare to find a smooth case 'box with a perfectly slick change and, if you do, it will quickly be ruined if any more than standard 948 power and gentle use is expected. It's a common upgrade, then, to exchange this 'smooth case' gearbox for a later 'ribbed case' 1098 'box.

Although this swap is not difficult or particularly expensive, there are a few things to take into account. The clutch release fork differs between the 948 and 1098 cars, to compensate for the different thickness of engine backplate (the 948 item is pressed steel, whereas the 1098

948 gear sticks (bottom) are shorter than 1098 items (top) and the two should not be interchanged.

948 'smooth case' gearbox is externally similar to the 803 'box but with a remote change.

Note the strengthening ribs on this 1098 gearbox. This casing is shared with Spridget 1275 'boxes.

engine was fitted with a ¼-inch thick lump of steel plate). The flywheel (thicker and heavier on 948 cars) and clutch (smaller diameter for early cars) also differ.

If a 1098 gearbox is to be fitted behind a 948 engine, it is recommended to upgrade to the later clutch and fly-wheel, which also means fitting a thicker, 1098-style back-plate and retaining the later release fork from the 1098 gearbox to operate the clutch. Now is also a good time to check and replace, if necessary, the crankshaft spigot bush which supports the front end of the gearbox input shaft.

1098 GEARBOX

This 'ribbed case' gearbox is the strongest of those fitted to the Minor by the factory. It sat behind the 1098cc engine on all Minors produced after 1962. Identifiable by a series of strengthening ribs, the 1098 gearbox features improved synchromesh over the 803 and 948 gearboxes, utilising a separate baulk ring instead of the cone-type syncros fitted to these earlier 'boxes.

Note the difference in depth between the 803/948-type clutch release bearing (left) and the later 1098-type. Note that forks differ as well.

MG Midgets also used a ribbed case gearbox behind their 1275 engines, which is a straight swap for the Minor 'box but uses closer ratios for better acceleration and needle roller bearings on second and third gears. This is a much more robust design than the Minor gear-box's bronze bushes, far better suited to higher-output engines. The clutch release fork from a Morris Minor gearbox will be required for one of these 'boxes to be fitted, however, as the Spridgets used a hydraulic clutch set-up as standard.

5-SPEED UPGRADES

The Minor's original gearbox/final drive set-up means that the engine is running at high revs if required to keep up with modern traffic on dual carriageways. Although changing the final drive ratio (*see* later) can help to reduce revs at high speed, at the other end of the spectrum, acceleration will be stunted and the engine and clutch both put under more strain accelerating from lower speeds. The solution, of course, is to equip your Minor with another gear for high-speed cruising, without blunting bottom-end performance. Enter the five-speed gearbox which, in response to the development of the motorway network and a need for cars to travel faster for longer, became a ubiquitous fitment to new cars not long after Morris Minor production finished.

The Type-9 Gearbox

The Ford Type 9 gearbox conversion remains the most popular of the five-speed gearbox conversions fitted to Morris Minors, and kits are readily available for its fitment. The conversion kit includes a cast aluminium bellhousing, clutch friction plate to match the type 9's input shaft splines, spigot bush to support the input shaft, propshaft, gearbox crossmember and a fibreglass transmission cover to replace the pressed steel original, as well as other brackets and sundries. Some kits include a clutch linkage which allows the retention of the original type mechanical clutch (although some owners opt to fit a hydraulic clutch kit while undertaking this modification), whereas others specify that a hydraulic clutch must be used.

Conversion kits do not normally include the gearbox. However, these remain relatively easily available both on the second-hand market and reconditioned from specialist suppliers. Instructions are provided with the conversion kits, which are essential for successful fitting. Kits differ depending on the manufacturer/supplier, with the rear cross-member particularly worthy of note. Many kits use a hybrid cross-member which is designed to mount in the original cross-member's position and utilise the same captive nuts in the chassis leg; however, this style mount has been known to fail over time, due to the additional weight of the gearbox and leverage on the mounting points. JLH Morris Minors offer a cross-member that

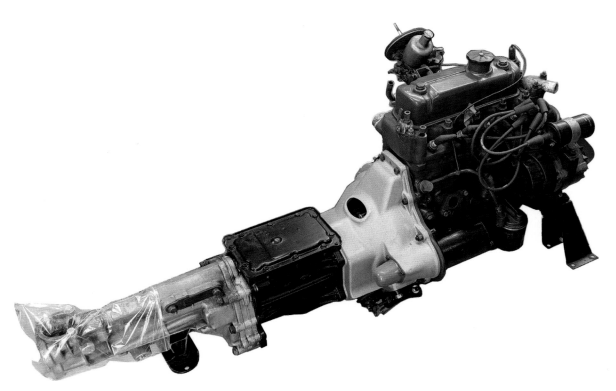

Ford's 'Type 9' gearbox, as fitted to the Ford Sierra, is a common and straightforward enough conversion for the Minor.

Type-9 conversion kits contain everything required for the conversion, apart from the 'box itself. Note the replacement fibreglass transmission cover which relocated the gear stick position further back than standard. The handbrake will require cutting down.

Barratt Engineering have developed this Suzuki-based kit for the MG Midget and plan to make a similar conversion available for the Minor soon.

utilises weld-on mounting points which eliminated this problem. At the time of writing, this cross-member is priced at £55 and is certainly worth considering when planning your conversion.

The Type-9's gearstick enters the Minor's cabin slightly further back than the original 'box (hence the need for the aftermarket fibreglass tunnel cover), necessitating the shortening of the Minor's original handbrake lever to clear the gear lever when in fourth gear. This is a relatively straightforward modification and is detailed in the instructions supplied with the fitting kit.

Note that the type-9 gearbox was never fitted with an oil drain plug, only a filler on the side of the 'box. However, with the propshaft removed it is likely that the oil will have leaked out of the third motion shaft seal where the propshaft is fitted in use. It makes sense while the 'box is out to drain it fully, either from here or the filler plug, and replace both input and tail shaft seals while it is easily accessible on the bench. 1.9 litres of semi-synthetic 75W90 oil is specified for refilling. Keep the box topped up to the level of the fill plug when the car is level.

A New Alternative?

UK-based Barratt engineering have recently (at the time of writing) unveiled their conversion kits, which allow a 5-speed Suzuki gearbox to be bolted to the back of an A-series engine. The first kit on offer is designed with the MG Midget in mind, but the author understands that work is underway on a version of the kit to suit the Morris Minor. This is certainly a development worth keeping a close eye on as it progresses. Click to www.barrattengineering.co.uk to find out more.

CLUTCH OPTIONS

948

The 948 flywheel is heavy, allowing for a low, smooth idle, and the clutch smaller than the 1098 item.

1098

A larger-diameter flywheel and clutch was introduced along with the 1098 engine and ribbed-case gearbox.

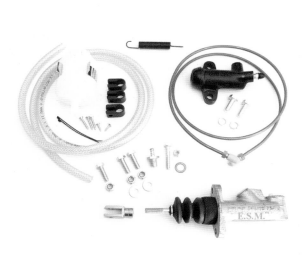

Hydraulic clutch kits are available and particularly beneficial if the clutch pressure plate has been upgraded.

Ford Sierra 1.6 pressure plate fits directly onto the Minor's flywheel and offers superior clamping force. A roller release bearing is required, however.

Note that this hydraulic clutch master cylinder is fitted to the remnants of the original gearbox cross-member which has, in this instance, been cut down to accommodate a type-9 5-speed gearbox. Solid copper pipe has been used in place of the kit-supplied flexible pipe from the remote reservoir.

Midget

As mentioned previously, the MG Midget's crankshaft uses a six-stud bolt pattern with offset dowels to locate the flywheel. Although a converted 1098 flywheel for the Marina crankshaft is available, it may only be used if one of the locating dowels is removed. If you are on a budget, it may be desirable to use the flywheel and clutch originally fitted to the MG Midget in your Minor, although this is not common practice.

Sierra

A Ford Sierra 1.6 clutch pressure plate may be used to offer additional pressure over the standard 1098 item. It fits directly onto the standard 1098 flywheel and its additional spring pressure is useful if your engine is producing significantly more power than standard. It should be noted, however, that as this is a diaphragm-type clutch, a roller release bearing must be used.

Hydraulic clutch

A hydraulic clutch kit may be desired to replace the mechanical linkage, especially if a heavier sprung pressure plate is fitted. Kits are available for this conversion that consist of a master cylinder mounted to the gearbox cross-member on the inside of the chassis leg, a reservoir to be mounted in the engine bay, pipework and a slave cylinder to be fitted to the side of the gearbox to actuate the clutch release arm. Note that five-speed gearbox conversions may require a different kit, or the kit adapting to fit, depending on the bellhousing used. Consult the vendor before purchasing the kit if you are unsure.

Note: Before splashing out on a hydraulic clutch kit, first check that your mechanical linkage is in good order. Wear is common and replacement of the OE set-up is far more straightforward and much cheaper than converting to hydraulic as a sticking plaster solution.

Gearbox Swaps at a Glance

Engine	Gearbox	Backplate	Flywheel	Clutch	Release Fork
948	Smooth case	Pressed steel	Thick 948 type	948 type	948 type
948	Ribbed case	Thick plate, 1098-type	1098-tube	1098-type	1098-type
1098	Smooth case	Pressed steel	Thick 948 type	948 type	948 type
1098	Ribbed case	Thick plate, 1098-type	1098-tube	1098-type	1098-type
1275 Midget	Ribbed case	Thick plate, 1098-type	Re-drilled 1098 (Esm code 10M001SCK) with one locating stud removed (see 'Midget' notes above)	1098-type	1098-type
1275 Marina	Ribbed case	Thick plate, 1098-type	Re-drilled 1098	1098-type	1098-type
1098	Type 9 5-spd	1098	Standard 1098	1098 pressure plate with 5-speed friction plate	1098-type
1275	Type 9 5-spd	1098	Re-drilled 1098	1098 or Sierra pressure plate (see 'Sierra' notes above) with 5-speed friction plate	1098-type. Note: Roller release bearing required for Sierra clutch

7

Final Drive and Differential Differences

The standard live rear axle fitted to all post-MM Series cars is known as an 'A-Series' axle and shares common components with a number of other cars in the BMC range, including the MG Midget, Austin A30 and A35, Riley One-Point-Five and Wolseley 1500. It consists of a steel casing, front-loading differential unit (*see* note below), a pair of half shafts (driven shafts, one per side, which transfer power from the differential gears to the driven wheels), hubs with bearings and brakes (7-inch diameter drum brakes on all Minor variants).

The final drive unit is housed in an aluminium casing, which is bolted to the front of the Minor's live rear axle.

A note on differentials: The differential is the clever arrangement of gears that allows one driven wheel to move faster than the other, necessary when cornering, as naturally the outer wheel travels further than the inner wheel. Common parlance includes the hypoid gears known as the crownwheel and pinion in the overall 'differential' term, and you will often hear final drive ratios (the relationship between the number of teeth on the pinion divided by the number of teeth on the crown wheel) referred to as differential ratios, although this is not strictly the correct terminology.

UNDERSTANDING 'DIFF' SWAPS – FAST OR QUICK?

Top speed and acceleration can be altered by changing the final drive ratio either by increasing or decreasing the overall rolling radius of the road wheel/tyre or by changing the differential unit for one with a different final drive ratio. In basic terms, a lower (sometimes referred to as taller) final drive ratio provides a higher top speed, whereas a higher (shorter) gear ratio provides quicker acceleration but a lower top speed.

From standard, a 948-powered Morris Minor will have been fitted with a 4.55:1 final drive (identifiable by the filler plug on the side of the aluminium casing), and a 1098-powered Minor a 4.22:1 final drive. Note that if an originally 948-powered Minor is to be fitted with a later differential unit (4.22:1, 3.9:1 or 3.7:1), it will be necessary either to drill the axle casing and weld in place a threaded collar for a filler plug in the correct place on

Markings on the crown wheel and/or differential housing denote ratio. In this case 38/9 = 4.2222 so the ratio is 4.22:1

the axle casing to replicate the later axle; swap the axle casing in its entirety for a later unit; or, simply fill the axle with a pre-measured quantity of oil through the breather tube or with one half-shaft removed. The latter is clearly not an ideal solution, and it does not offer the opportunity for the axle oil level to be checked; however, it may prove useful to those working on a trial and error approach to settling on a final drive ratio that suits you and your car.

The MG Midget, with its 13-inch wheels and 1275 engine, was fitted with a 3.9:1 ratio final drive, which is commonly fitted to Minors' top lower revs for high-speed cruising. Similarly, late 1500 Midgets and Riley One-Point Five and Wolseley 1500 cars used a 3.7:1 final drive, which some Minor owners have chosen to fit if they travel many miles on the motorway network.

As mentioned previously, this gearing is great for fast running, but the Minor will not be quick off the mark and may struggle with hills. A 3.7:1 final drive is only really worth considering if your Minor is fitted with a more powerful engine and you do not, for whatever reason, wish to fit a five-speed gearbox, which removes the need for compromise.

Note that changing the final drive ratio will also affect the accuracy of the speedometer, which takes its drive from the third motion shaft of the gearbox. In the short term, GPS speedometers, or even mobile phone apps, are cheap and simple solutions; however, once you are fully committed to the differential fitted to your car, there are companies, such as Speedy Cables in Swansea (www.speedycables.com), who will be able to recalibrate your original speedometer head for you. Alternatively, the speedometer head, or just the mechanism if the original facia is desired, could be swapped for a unit from a Minor that would have used the chosen final drive ratio from standard. Alternatively, for those looking to push the boat out, electronic speedometers that replicate the original Smiths' unit perfectly are now available, using GPS for their speed sensing, despatching with the speedometer cable altogether. They are expensive, but well worth considering if you want an accurate speedometer in your Minor and are considering future changes to your final drive ratio.

REAR AXLE UPGRADES

If serious power upgrades are to be considered, it is worth noting that the sun and planet gear 'open' differential units nestled within the final drive assemblies of all standard Morris Minors can be swapped for limited-slip

Standard A-series differentials are not the strongest, so for serious power upgrades, an upgraded rear axle or limited slip differential unit is a sensible option, as this ruined unit from the author's supercharged Minor proves.

versions (known as LSDs) for fast road or motorsport purposes. These differentials are stronger than the standard items, which can fail if excessive power is to be considered. To the same end, competition half-shafts manufactured from EN24 steel (*see* www.petermayengineering.com) are a sensible upgrade over the standard shafts if hard use or increased power is intended.

Ford Escort, Triumph Dolomite (and Dolomite Sprint) and MGB axles have all been successfully fitted to Morris Minors in the past with some modification and are all capable of taking more power and abuse than the standard Minor axle. The use of an alternative axle, however, will change the Pitch Circle Diameter (PCD) and require a change of wheels at least on the rear axle, with implications including the requirement to create two spare wheels (*see* notes on PCD changes in the next chapter). The Escort axle uses 100mm PCD hubs, whereas the Dolomite axle uses 3.75-inch PCD hubs and the MGB uses 4.5-inch PCD hubs. If a rear axle upgrade is desired, it is sensible to change the front hubs at the same time. 100mm PCD hubs are available to suit several of the Ford-based disc brake conversions on the market, the Morris Marina originally used 3.75-inch PCD hubs and therefore Marina hubs may be used alongside Marina-based disc brake conversions on the front. Marina vans used 4.5-inch PCD, so (if you can find them) these hubs may be used alongside Marina disc brakes to convert the PCD to 4.5 inch all round. Suitable wheels will then require sourcing.

8

Wheels and Tyres

If we are to consider brake and suspension upgrades to the Morris Minor, first we must consider the four Post-it note-sized contact patches where rubber meets road. A great number of wheel options, from the standard 3J steel wheels to a variety of alloy wheels are available, but tyre choice should be given at least as much consideration as the wheels on which they sit.

NOTE: If you change your wheels, you may also need to change your wheel nut type. If you opt to use a standard Morris Minor wheel as a spare, be sure to carry a set of standard Minor wheel nuts to suit should the need to use it ever arise.

STANDARD WHEELS

The Minor's standard 3J (three inches wide when measured between the inner edges of the wheel), 14-inch diameter wheels are incredibly narrow by today's standards but can still perform well for modest usage when shod with appropriate rubber.

Original specification was a 520-14 Dunlop crossply tyre, which is no longer available. Crossply tyres are not conducive to daily use anyway, and unless concourse level originality is desired, are best avoided in favour of a more modern radial construction tyre. The closest radial alternative to the original specification crossply is a 145/14, although the overall inflated diameter of these tyres is very slightly smaller than the original crossply on account of a shorter sidewall. The effective rolling radius of a proper period 145R14 is extremely close, however.

Choice of correctly fitting 145 radial tyres has been limited in recent years, leading to many owners fitting oversize 155/80/14 tyres to standard, narrow, wheels. These are closer to the original rolling radius, but are too wide for a standard rim and can seriously upset the handling characteristics of the car.

Bridgestone have offered a 145/80/14 with a modern tread pattern for some years. However, a more recent addition to the market is the Pirelli Cinturato, developed

145 Pirelli Cinturato (left) has an effective rolling radius extremely close to the OE-spec crossply (right).

by classic tyres specialist Longstone Tyres, specifically for the Morris Minor. Effectively, the Pirelli is taller with a thinner tread pattern. Designed to replicate the Dunlop 520-14, this is a modern tyre with a classic tread pattern and uncluttered sidewall designed specifically for the Minor's original wheels and therefore an option that is well-worth considering when choosing rubber for your Morris Minor.

It is also worth noting that inner tubes should be fitted to all standard Minor wheels, as there is no safety bead incorporated into the design of the wheel. A safety bead, as incorporated into the design of all modern wheels – including reproduction Minor van wheels (*see* later) – prevents the tyre from coming off the wheel's edges in the event of sudden deflation.

VAN WHEELS

Whether for performance or aesthetics, many owners choose to fit wider wheels to their Morris Minor. One of the most popular changes, and one favoured by the author on all three of his own Morris Minors, is the replacement of the standard 3J wheels with 4.5J versions as fitted to Morris Minor Light Commercial Vehicles (LCVs). ESM Morris Minors now reproduce these wheels with a mild design revision to include a modern tyre safety bead, allowing tyres to be fitted without the need for inner tubes.

Available off the shelf, powder-coated and ready to fit, these wheels are in keeping with the Minor's original aesthetic and can make a huge difference to the way a Minor handles when teamed with good tyres. It is possible to fit the Pirelli Cinturatos mentioned previously to these wheels without over stretching the sidewall. At the time of writing, Longstone tyres even offer the option of purchasing a set of Cinturatos to be delivered fitted to a brand new set of these 4.5J van wheels ready to fit to your car.

An alternative 4.5J wheel with the same centre and rims but a different offset was fitted to some 8cwt commercials. This offset difference has the effect of putting the outer edge of the wheel much further towards the outside of the car, offering increased clearance on the top trunnion at the front and filling the arches in an aesthetically pleasing way both at the front and rear (although they may stick out too far at the front if disc brakes are fitted, due to the difference in hub offset from standard drums). These wheels are highly desirable and are not currently being reproduced. They are identifiable by the part stamp 'LP917'.

BANDED STEEL WHEELS

Banding is the process of cutting a steel wheel in two then welding a strip of metal between the two halves to create a wider wheel. This is clearly a major engineering challenge and, although the result can be quite striking when complete, it is a job which must be carried out by an experienced specialist engineer on a jig to avoid the wheel warping during the welding process.

Reproduction van wheels offer a little additional width without looking out of place. Note the plain LCV hubcaps fitted here are directly interchangeable with car hubcaps which incorporate an 'M' motif.

Reproduction van wheels (right) are not only wider than standard car wheels (left) but also incorporate a safety bead, meaning that inner tubes are not required.

Banded steel wheels can look great, but make sure they have been banded safely.

Second-hand banded wheels represent a risk, without knowledge of how well the banding process was carried out. If a weld fails in service, the results can be catastrophic.

Although standard Minor wheels can be – and regularly are – banded, the lack of a safety bead means that inner tubes should still be used in the wider wheel. It may, therefore, be desirable to source a set of reproduction van wheels that incorporate the safety bead into their design, as the basis for the banding process. (For example, ESM Morris Minors often sell 'B-stock' wheels, which have a slightly less than perfect surface finish.)

ALLOY WHEELS

There are, of course, those who prefer an alloy wheel and here the choice becomes more varied. One of the most important things to consider when looking for a set of alloy wheels for your Morris Minor is the Pitch Circle Diameter, or PCD (distance between hole centres). On standard Minor hubs, this is 4 inches (101.6mm). Note that many alloy wheels, including many Ford wheels, use similar but not interchangeable 100mm PCD. Although it may be possible to physically fit these to the Minor's hubs,

14-inch Minilite style wheels are a popular fitment.

15-inch Minilite-style wheels fill the arches nicely with a lower-profile tyre.

to do so is not safe and can lead to snapped wheel studs and lost wheels.

Note: Early Minors (Series MM) featured a 4.5inch-PCD, the same as many Triumphs as well as MGBs.

The most common choice of alternative wheels with a 4-inch PCD is the Minilite, or Minilite-style 'Minator' wheel. These are generally available in 13-, 14- and 15-inch diameters and a range of offsets and widths. MG Midget 13-inch steel or Rostyle wheels also fit the Minor's 4-inch PCD.

Consider clearance on calipers if converting to smaller wheels as well as disc brakes. Test-fit a wheel to your car, ideally before committing to purchase, but certainly before spending money having wheels refurbished and/ or shod with new rubber.

PCD CHANGES

From standard, the Minor has a 4-stud, 4-inch (101.6mm-PCD) often referred to as 4x4inch. It is possible, however, to convert the PCD of your Minor to open up a wider range of wheels, or to find wheels to suit a preferred axle or front hub set-up with a non-standard PCD.

In days gone by, the latter would have been a common occurrence, as disc brake conversions gained popularity with hubs from either a Marina (3.75-inch PCD), Marina van (4.5-inch PCD), or Ford (100-mm PCD) were used. Often this led to either mismatched wheels front to rear (and two spare wheels being carried) or the need to fit an alternative axle – often Triumph Dolomite (3.75-inch PCD), MGB (4.5-inch PCD) or Ford Escort (108mm PCD) in order to match the rear PCD to the front hubs.

Nowadays, there are a good number of nicely engineered disc brake conversions that feature either new or re-worked hubs, which suit the disc brake conversion while retaining the Minor's original 4-inch PCD.

If you have bought an already non-standard Minor, it is worth considering what modifications have been fitted and the implications thereof before considering fitting upgrades of your own. MGB and Austin Cambridge wheels are 4.5-inch PCD, Marina and Triumph Dolomite wheels are 3.75-inch, and there is a huge range of wheels on the market with a 108mm PCD to satisfy the aftermarket wheel market for Ford cars and others which use this common PCD.

9

Drum Brake Modifications

It is all very well making your Morris Minor go better, but first it is essential to make sure it can stop on demand, too. As we discussed in the chapter on servicing your Minor, a well set-up and regularly maintained set of drum brakes, particularly the later 8-inch front drums fitted to the Minor 1000 along with the larger 1098cc engine for the 1962 model year, are perfectly adequate for daily use.

However, there are clear advantages to upgrading your braking system to both improve performance, including reducing brake fade associated with drum brakes which can struggle to cool as effectively as discs, but also reduce the amount of maintenance required to keep braking performance where it needs to be. The improved performance of disc brakes becomes essential as speeds increase, and also makes driving on modern roads with cars which, from standard, pull up far quicker than the Minor, a safer proposition.

In the chapters that follow we will discuss the various options available to you when it comes to upgrading your Minor's brakes. It should first be considered, however, that the key to success here is in purchasing quality components, shoes and pads in particular, as well as in ensuring that the rest of the braking system is in good order. A master cylinder with leaky seals will, of course, not push fluid to the slave cylinders or calipers effectively; likewise, a damaged/bulging flexi hose will cause the system to lose pressure. Maladjusted drum brakes will also cause issues. Under-adjustment will result in a long pedal, at best, whereas over-adjusted shoes will drag, create heat, potentially boil any moisture content in the brake fluid, warp brake drums or damage shoes. Any air trapped in the system could result in multiple pumps of the pedal being required to achieve effective braking.

Finally, remember that often the best brake upgrade you can achieve on any car is to fit a quality set of tyres. The tiny contact patch at the base of the tyre at each corner is the car's only interface with the road. Good brakes are no good if the tyre cannot grip the road and simply lock up. Consider fitting wider wheels to increase the size of this contact patch, but also consider carefully the quality of rubber that surrounds them. Turn back to Chapter 8 to learn more.

LARGER DRUMS

If your Morris Minor is fitted with the early-type 7-inch drum brakes fitted prior to 1962 (excluding the very early 'MM'-type brakes), it is an incredibly straightforward task

Riley One-Point-Five brakes offer improved stopping power over the Minor's drums, however parts availability is an issue.

to swap the backplates, shoes, springs and drums for a post-'62 8-inch set-up. Of course, unless they are in perfect condition, it makes sense to replace the wheel cylinders, fixings and link pipe at the same time. Although almost everything for this conversion is available brand new off the shelf, the backplates are not, and so second-hand items will need to be sourced. So common is the conversion of later cars to disc brake set-ups, however, that finding a second-hand set of 8-inch backplates should neither be difficult nor expensive. Keep your eyes peeled on the Owners' Club web forum and social media channels, or visit rallies and autojumbles to find what you need. The Morris Minor-owning community are a good bunch and always ready to help where they can.

Even larger drum brakes were fitted to other cars in the BMC stable, with both the Riley 1.5 and Wolseley 1500 being fitted with 9-inch drums that can be bolted directly onto the standard Minor kingpin. It should be noted that, although the same diameter as one another and sharing the same kingpin, Riley and Wolseley drum brake set-ups differ from one another and most parts are not interchangeable between the two. The Riley set-up is from Girling, whereas the Wolseley uses Lockheed brakes. Wolseley brakes are narrower than the Riley set-up and are regarded as better suited to the Minor. Wolseley brakes can be identified as having an adjuster accessible through a hole in the brake drum, as on the Minor, whereas the Riley brakes are adjusted via a cam driven from the rear of the backplate.

Upgrading to either Riley or Wolseley drum brakes used to be fairly common practice for Morris Minor owners looking for a little additional stopping power; however, in recent years, parts availability and cost for these set-ups have pushed the cost of the conversion higher and higher, and with the availability of a number of off-the-shelf disc brake conversions at reasonable prices with good spares availability, the 9-inch drum conversion has very much fallen out of favour.

That said, if you are able to source a Wolseley set-up, some owners have reported that with some modification to the backplate, Minor wheel cylinders can be fitted, reducing the cost and improving the availability of parts for future maintenance. Both Wolseley and Riley brake shoes will likely require re-lining, however, when the friction material wears as availability of off-the-shelf replacement shoes is limited.

FIT A SERVO

Whether your Morris Minor is fitted with drum brakes or discs, the addition of a servo will not improve your braking, per se; however, it will make it easier for more force to be applied through the pedal to the calipers/wheel cylinders. An in-line vacuum-operated servo is a relatively cheap and simple bolt-on modification that will reduce the amount of effort required to push the brake pedal in order to provide effective braking. However, a servo should never be used as a sticking plaster solution to mask a poorly maintained and ineffectual braking system.

The Minor's standard brake plumbing splits the feeds to the front and rear brakes by means of a banjo bolt at the rear of the master cylinder. For a remote servo to act upon

A brake servo is a commonly misunderstood upgrade. It reduces the amount of pedal pressure required, but does not improve stopping power.

Servo kits are available for the Minor, which include fitting instructions, pipework and bracketry required.

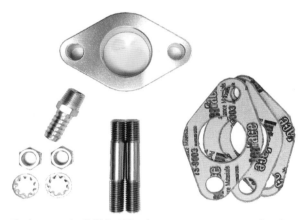

If using a standard HS2 (or H2) carburettor, servo vacuum may be taken via a carburettor spacer (ESM part number CBS115C).

Alternatively, a vacuum take-off should be installed in the inlet manifold.

inlet manifold in place of the original bakelite spacer – an elegant solution. A non-return valve is recommended in the vacuum line between the inlet manifold and the servo.

Servo kits are available from marque specialists including ESM Morris Minors, and are supplied with fitting instructions and guidance on orientation. Brake line kits are also available, pre-fitted with the required ends for the installation.

SILICONE FLUID

Conventional DOT 4 brake fluid is glycol-based and is hygroscopic. This means that it absorbs moisture from the air and should, therefore, be changed every three years to prevent the fluids incompressibility and high boiling point being compromised by water absorbed in the system.

Another key issue of conventional fluid's hygroscopic nature is that the thin film of fluid which is left on the cylinder walls of the hydraulic components in the braking system will also attract moisture from the air and cause corrosion. This can seize components or compromise the smoothness of critical mating surfaces, resulting in leaks

all four wheels, the master cylinder must be re-plumbed so that it feeds the servo inlet directly, with the front-to-rear split taken after the servo outlet.

A vacuum feed to the servo will also be required. After-market manifolds often include a drilled and tapped hole as standard, either with an outlet already fitted or a blank which can be removed and replaced with a hose fitting. If your standard manifold is to be modified, it is highly recommended that it is removed from the engine and drilled/tapped on the bench to prevent the risk of swarf being sucked into the engine. Alternatively, a pre-drilled spacer plate (ESM part number CBS155C) may be fitted between the standard H2 or HS2 carburettor and

DOT 5 silicone brake fluid will not absorb water from the air as is the case with DOT 4.

ture, protecting the components in the braking system from corrosion and thus increasing their life expectancy significantly.

BRAIDED HOSES

Originally, three flexible rubber brake hoses were used on the Minor – one each side at the front from the solid brake pipes at the inner wing to the brake drums on the front swivels, and one between the axle and master cylinder to the rear hard line, just above the propshaft mounting flange.

These rubber hoses can break down over time and leak, swell, become corroded on their mid-steel ferrules or otherwise deteriorate to the point of being dangerous and/or MOT failure points.

If replacing these, or carrying out other work to your Minor's brake hydraulic system, it makes sense to upgrade to a (theoretical) fit-and-forget solution which should improve braking efficiency, too.

Braided brake hoses, available for the Minor from a number of manufacturers and suppliers, feature an inner hose (often made of Teflon), which is surrounded by a stainless steel braided sheath. This serves both to protect the inner hose and prevent the swelling effect often found in even thick-walled rubber hoses.

Due to this lack of swelling and consequently improved braking efficiency, it is essential that if one front hose is to be replaced with a braided hose, then both should be. However, as the system will require bleeding anyway, it makes sense to replace all three as a set.

and potentially, on a car such as the Minor with a single circuit braking system, complete brake failure.

The solution is to upgrade to an initially more expensive silicone fluid, which should be maintenance free and protect the braking system from damage. Silicone fluid is actively hydrophobic, which means that it repels mois-

Braided brake hoses are, theoretically, fit and forget. Do keep an eye on them for signs of damage or deterioration, however.

10

Convert to Disc Brakes

There are several advantages of disc brakes over drums, which is why disc brakes have become ubiquitous on modern cars, while drums are reserved nowadays for the rear brakes on cheap runarounds only. Several conversion kits, and variations on a theme, are available to upgrade your Minor to this modern braking system. However, there are a few other things to consider first before bolting on a kit.

The brake master cylinder must be modified to allow the caliper pistons to return without pressure being held in the system; provision must be made for increased fluid capacity by means of a remote reservoir which should be installed; and consideration should be given as to whether a remote servo (*see* previous chapter) should be fitted to reduce the required pedal pressure.

As is the case for modifications using a drum brake set-up, braided hoses and conversion to silicone fluid are worth considering. The most critical point of all is that the braking system should be in good working order and upgrades not used simply to mask poor performance due to maladjustment, air in the system, old brake fluid, seized wheel cylinders, contaminated brake linings or an ailing master cylinder.

MODIFYING THE MASTER CYLINDER FOR DISC BRAKES

If you are to fit disc brakes to your Morris Minor, first the master cylinder must be removed from the car and modified by removing the 'top hat' seal, also known as the 'valve cup', which serves to retain pressure in a drum-braked set-up to allow the disc brake calipers' pistons to return fully. Failure to do this would result in the front brakes sticking on, or 'dragging'.

Removal of the master cylinder is a fairly involved process and one which many regard as the most awkward of any job on a Morris Minor. Located in the driver's side chassis leg, the cylinder is accessed by removing the front carpet and master cylinder cover plate, which is held in place by a number of brass set screws. The cylinder must

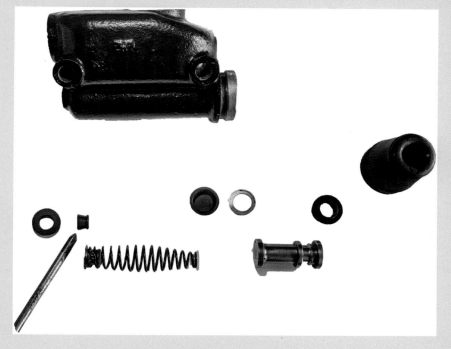

Valve cup seal (known as a top hat seal) should be removed if disc brakes are to be fitted.

A used master cylinder should be rebuilt and its cylinder wall carefully and thoroughly cleaned before reassembly with new seals.

cases, abrasion here could result in the propagation of a crack which could fracture the torsion bar.

With the cross-bolts removed, the master cylinder may be levered forward against the floorpan edge allowing the $\frac{7}{16}$ AF spanner to once again be utilised to partially slacken the pipe union on the rear of the brake banjo before a $\frac{5}{8}$ UNF spanner can be deployed to remove the banjo from the back of the master cylinder. Note that two copper washers are present here and will need to be replaced as a matter of course. Finally, the master cylinder can be withdrawn from the chassis leg, noting the condition of the pushrod and its yolk on the brake pedal, which should be replaced if bent or significantly corroded, as is often the case.

Given the involved nature of removing the cylinder, it would be foolish not to either completely rebuild the master cylinder at this point with a new set of seals (a rebuild kit is around £10 at the time of writing), or replace the master cylinder in its entirety, modifying the replacement part for use with disc brakes straight out of the box. Note that a genuine master cylinder must be used if converting to disc brakes, as the cheaper pattern-type cylinders are unsuitable for conversion for use with the remote reservoir. The latter is required to allow sufficient fluid capacity to compensate for the increased displacement of fluid by the caliper pistons, as pads wear when compared to the relatively small displacement of the standard wheel cylinders, in which adjustment of the snail cam compensated for brake shoe wear.

A replacement cylinder will have a perfect bore and fresh seals, so is often regarded as the safer option; however, if a rebuild is the desired course of action, this is not a difficult task. Nevertheless, there are a few points to consider throughout the process. Any wear or corrosion to the cylinder's internal bore will immediately damage new seals or provide a valley through which brake fluid may pass, bypassing the seals and reducing braking effort. This internal bore serves as a working surface for the master cup and secondary cup rubber seals and must be in perfect unworn and uncorroded condition to avoid the risk of brake failure due to the seals being damaged by any abrasive lip. Similarly, any detritus floating in the reservoir has the potential to enter the cylinder and cause damage to seals. As such, if the internals of the casting are heavily pitted or corroded (not unlikely due to the hygroscopic nature of conventional brake fluid), a replacement master cylinder will almost certainly be necessary.

Whether using a new part or your original master cylinder, stripdown and re-assembly is a straightforward task

first be emptied by means of a syringe and/or pumped out via a bleed nipple on one of the wheel cylinders and the old fluid disposed of in an environmentally friendly manner. Next, the plumbing to the cylinder must be released. Working from beneath the car, a $\frac{7}{16}$ AF spanner may be used to release the front brake feed union from the banjo at the rear of the master cylinder and, while under the car, the master cylinder cross-bolts that secure the cylinder to the chassis may be removed. From the factory, these bolts were fitted before the torsion bars and so require either the bar to be removed or, more commonly, gently bent out of the way by means either of a G-clamp or a lever to allow the bolt to pass through. Alternatively, some owners opt to simply slice the head off the bolts with an angle grinder to facilitate their removal. On re-assembly, it is advisable to refit the bolts the opposite way around (with plenty of copper grease on their shafts to prevent seizure in the cylinder); however, it should be noted that shallow nuts should be used and the bolts shortened sufficiently so as to avoid contact with the torsion bar. In extreme that is well within the capabilities of most home mechanics, so long as care is taken not to damage seals or lose parts of the cylinder as spring tension is released.

First, ensure the master cylinder is empty of fluid. If the original cylinder is to be re-used, position a number of rags around the cylinder outlets to catch any remaining fluid that may be ejected as the piston is depressed. Wear eye protection, too, as brake fluid is a corrosive substance and should be handled with care. Clamp the master cylinder in a vice, positioned with the drain plug end facing downwards. Remove the rubber pushrod boot, then use a parallel punch or screwdriver to depress the piston (take care to avoid any escaping fluid). Next, with the piston still depressed, use a pair of circlip pliers to remove the retaining clip at the front of the assembly. Gently release pressure on the piston (be prepared for the components to spring out – hold a rag over the top to catch anything ejected at speed) and collate the internal components.

If a new cylinder is being used, simply remove the 'top hat' valve cup and reassemble (using a little brake fluid of the type to be used – *see* the earlier text on silicone fluid) as an assembly lubricant. Alternatively, a proprietary brake cylinder assembly lube or red rubber grease may be used. This is especially advisable if the cylinder is not to be immediately fitted, as conventional DOT 4 fluid may attract moisture from the air and cause corrosion to the cylinder wall in storage.

If refurbishing a pre-enjoyed master cylinder, a few checks and additional processes must be carried out. Firstly, every component must be scrupulously clean. Carefully remove the master and secondary cup seals from the piston using a small screwdriver, taking care not to mark the piston or to impale your fingers in the process.

It is likely that the rearmost seal, the valve washer, will have remained in the bottom of the cylinder. Remove it carefully with a pick or bent piece of wire, taking care not to mark the cylinder wall in the process. Remove the filler and drain plugs.

Clean the now-bare casting thoroughly, then inspect the cylinder bore for wear, corrosion and damage. If heavily pitted or scored, the cylinder will need to be replaced; however, light corrosion or a small wear step in the bore may be carefully rectified as follows.

Mix up a rust removal solution and submerge the master cylinder in it for the time specified on the product you choose. Fine marks can be removed by means of a Scotch-Brite pad. An aluminium welding rod with one end bent 180 degrees and a small piece of Scotch-Brite tucked into the hook serves as a perfect mandrell to be used in a cordless drill for this process, as the soft aluminium is unlikely to damage the cylinder wall if it comes into contact with it. Wearing eye protection, turn this home-made honing tool slowly in a cordless drill working in and out, up and down the cylinder. This may be done with the cylinder partially submerged in the rust removal solution, if you are careful to avoid splashing of this acidic solution for best effect. If wear remains, miniature sprung stone honing tools that fit into a cordless drill can be purchased for this purpose. Used slowly and with plenty of light oil, these offer a heavier cut than the Scotch-Brite and are often used to revive very worn cylinders on classics where replacement is not an option. This is a similar honing process to engine cylinder bores and can be incredibly effective if done correctly. In severe cases, cylinders may be bored out and fitted with a stainless steel sleeve; however, this is not common practice on Minor master cylinders, given the cost versus that of a brand new master cylinder.

Once the bores are free from pitting and wear, the cylinder must be thoroughly cleaned once again before reassembly can commence. If the cylinder is to be painted at this stage, it must be masked carefully to avoid paint making contact with any working surfaces or entering the fluid reservoir.

New seals must be fitted to the piston carefully to avoid damage to them, and in the orientation shown in the workshop manual, and finally the assembly may be reconstructed in the opposite manner to its earlier deconstruction, remembering that the 'top hat' valve cup must not be fitted if conversion to disc brakes is being considered.

It will also be necessary to fit a remote reservoir to keep the master cylinder topped up with fluid when converting to disc brakes. We will be covering this next, so do not fully reassemble and reinstall the master cylinder until you have given this full consideration and installed provision for it.

REMOTE RESERVOIR

As mooted previously, if you are to fit disc brakes to your Minor, a remote reservoir is necessary to provide sufficient surplus fluid to keep the master cylinder topped up when fluid is displaced behind the caliper pistons. These have a larger volumetric capacity than the Minor's standard wheel cylinders and also self-adjust as the brake pads, as opposed to the standard drum set-up, which utilises

A remote fluid reservoir must be fitted for disc brakes, but is a useful addition to a drum brake set-up for ease of maintenance.

manual snail cam adjusters that keep wheel cylinders working within the same range of movement throughout the life of the friction material.

A remote reservoir in the engine bay need not be reserved for only disc brake-equipped cars, however. The remote reservoir enables a quick visual check on brake fluid level from beneath the bonnet, a check so often neglected in the master cylinder's position beneath the driver's footwell carpet. Keeping a close check on brake fluid level will give you an early warning of any leaks developing before complete loss of fluid and brakes.

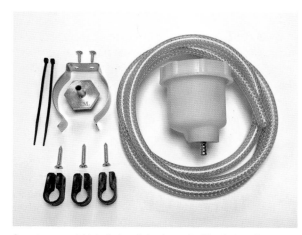

Remote reservoir kit includes all that is required for the installation, including a replacement master cylinder drain plug incorporating a filler tube.

Now fluid is entering the master cylinder from above, the vent hole in the original filler cap must be blanked to avoid the contents of the remote reservoir leaking through this. Non-vented caps are available specifically for this purpose; however, it is not a difficult job to blank the hole in an original vented cap. The author's preferred method for this is to drill and tap the original vent hole to 8BA, dip an 8BA set screw in chemical metal to provide a permanent seal, then screw this into the threaded hole. Note that the fibre washer below the filler cap now becomes even more important as a seal, and so must be replaced if in less than perfect condition.

Reinstalling the master cylinder is fiddly indeed, but the process is simply the reverse of its removal, noting the observation described previously that the master cylinder securing bolts should be replaced in the opposite orientation to their factory originals and that the flexible hose from the remote reservoir must be connected firmly to the adapted drain plug within the chassis leg. In the experience of the author, the easiest method for this re-assembly is to install the rear banjo union with its fresh copper washers loosely on the bench before introducing the master cylinder to the chassis leg.

The cylinder should be engaged on the pushrod and slid forward, so that the pushrod depresses the piston within the master cylinder and the rubber boot located onto the pushrod and cylinder grooves. With the cylinder held forward by means of a screwdriver or similarly slender lever, the rear brake pipe can be threaded (finger tight) into the rear of the banjo connector. A small cable tie wrapped tightly

Remote filler coupling replaces master cylinder drain plug. Note that this filler conversion is only compatible with genuine master cylinders, and not pattern ones.

around the brake pipe just behind the union is useful to prevent the union sliding back along the pipe out of reach into the chassis leg (note that this is an essential technique if this pipe is being replaced with new). The master cylinder can now be located into its final position and its cross-bolts installed. With the cylinder located, the front brake pipe that enters the banjo on the rear of the master cylinder via the side of the chassis leg can be installed, with the banjo

still loose enough that its position may be adjusted so that the threaded union is lined up perfectly with the hole in the chassis leg. The front pipe may now be tightened into the banjo fully, then the banjo connector tightened fully from the drivers' footwell by means of a ⅝ AF spanner. Finally, the rear brake pipe may be tightened fully.

When you are ready to introduce fluid to the system (consider upgrading to silicone fluid at this point), note that the remote reservoir should be filled first, then the master cylinder filler cap loosened until fluid starts to overflow, then tightened fully. This ensures that there is no airlock between the remote fluid reservoir and the fluid reservoir in the original cast cylinder.

DISC BRAKES – THE OPTIONS

Marina-based Disc Brake Conversion

Disc brake kits based on the Morris Marina set-up are a common and cost-effective upgrade. Using solid discs, uprated wheel hubs with taper roller bearings and a pair of twin-pot calipers, they improve braking performance greatly and are more than sufficient as an upgrade for most road use, with brake cooling much improved over the enclosed drum and a decent clamping force able to be exerted on the discs whether or not a remote servo has been installed in the system. (See Chapter 9.)

Marina-based disc brake conversion kit includes hubs based upon those originally fitted to the Marina, but with the Minor's 4-inch PCD.

The Marina set-up uses solid discs which can struggle to dissipate heat under very heavy use.

Ford-based vented disc conversion kit is available with both steel and alloy hubs.

Note: For increased pad area, it is possible to fit MGB calipers to the Marina conversion brackets, as they use the same offset and PCD as the Marina calipers, and give a much wider range of performance pad compounds, available through MG specialists such as MGOC Spares.

Ford Vented Conversion

Vented disc brakes allow better cooling, and are ideally suited to fast road or track use as well as for towing or simply the peace of mind that comes with having a more modern and effective braking set-up on your Minor. The Ford-based conversion kits available from a variety of specialists (ESM part number DSK100) offer a choice of aluminium or steel hubs, calipers, vented discs and all the hardware required for fitting. As with the Marina kit, the Minor's original 4x4-inch PCD is retained; however, a minimum of 14-inch wheels are required to clear the calipers. The Marina originally used 13-inch wheels. More expensive than the Marina-derived kit, the vented option undoubtedly offers better braking in hard use, so it is well worth considering if your driving style relies on brakes that will not fade with heavy use.

Vented discs cool much more efficiently than solid ones, and are
therefore less prone to warping. Alloy wheels help improve airflow to
the brakes.

The JLH 4-pot vented disc option offers some serious stopping power.

There are variations upon a theme. Consider the implications of
sourcing parts in the future if considering a low-volume kit, or putting
something together yourself.

JLH conversion

JLH Morris Minors – a company you will have heard
mentioned previously in this book and will do again –
offers upgrades aimed at the performance end of the
Minor modification spectrum. That said, there is no such
thing as brakes that are too good for road use, so do not
discount JLH's four-pot vented kit if budget allows. JLH
also offer 2-pot Ford-based kits with hubs available in
both Minor (4-inch) and Ford (108mm) PCD to suit your
chosen wheels and rear axle set-up (*see* notes on PCD
changes in Chapter 8). More information can be found
at www.jlhmorrisminors.co.uk.

General Advice on Fitting Disc Brakes

Whichever kit you go for, the fitting thereof will be
much the same. The Minor's kingpin will need stripping
of its brake drum, hub and brake backing plate. The
flexible hose from the inner wing will require replacing with a custom hose, included in the kits, to transfer
fluid from the Minor's original solid lines to the newly
fitted calipers.

A caliper mounting bracket and brake backplate/splash
shield will next need to be mounted to the kingpin before
the new hub, complete with new bearings packed with
fresh grease and the disc bolted up to it, can be fitted.

If your kit includes hubs with taper roller bearings, note
that the original torque setting for the central hub nut
must be ignored. These more modern bearings require
tightening until all play is eliminated, then loosened until
play is just perceptible, then the split pin installed through
the castellated hub nut. These bearings should be checked
and adjusted after a few miles have been covered.

Be aware that manufacturers often coat brake discs in a
thin film of wax or oil to prevent them rusting in storage.
This must be removed before fitting. The calipers may now
be mounted, along with their brake pads. A dry fit with

Never over-tighten taper roller bearings. They should be nipped up so play is just eliminated, no more.

the pads removed is a good idea initially to ensure that the disc is correctly offset, so that it runs centrally to the caliper. The flexible hose should be fitted and tightened to the caliper first (with a copper washer where required), then the free end fastened to the hole in the inner wing, such that the hose is not twisted when the wheels are in the straight ahead position. Ensure that there is sufficient slack in the hose that it is not pulled taut at full lock in either direction. The original copper brake pipe may now be fitted to the flexible hose and the system bled of air.

11

Suspension Modifications

The standard Minor is reasonably comfortable, and contemporary journalists praised its rack-and-pinion steering for its positive feel when compared with other cars of the time. However, if a more sporting driving style is to be adopted, there are a few tweaks that can simply and relatively cheaply be made to improve the handling of your Minor.

It is important to strike a balance, however, as a Minor that has been lowered too far, or its suspension stiffened too much, can be anything from uncomfortable to alarming to drive. In this chapter we will explore upgrading suspension bushes, adjusting ride height, changing spring rates and dampers, adding an anti-roll bar and various other tweaks that are commonly employed to make the Minor an improved proposition for a more spirited driving style.

Note that fitting any suspension upgrade incorrectly has the potential to cause the car to handle dangerously or unpredictably. If you are unsure of any element of the processes involved, it is advisable to seek out an experienced engineer who has tackled these modifications before. Most Morris Minor restoration specialists will have seen all of what follows before and so will be well placed to advise or undertake the conversion on your behalf.

POLYURETHANE BUSHES

The Minor left the factory with rubber suspension bushes all round. These are sacrificial components that require changing from time to time, but act to insulate the body shell of the car and its interior occupants from road noise and bump transmission from the suspension. The clutch relay shaft is also insulated by a bush with a bronze insert where it enters the chassis leg, bringing the total number of bushes in the Morris Minor to 27.

Due to the composition of modern rubber, aftermarket rubber bushes tend to degrade quite quickly, in the experience of the author and numerous owners and restorers interviewed for this publication. So, with the process of replacing them being somewhat labour intensive, it makes sense to consider more modern alternatives that should give a longer service life when replacing them. Enter polyurethane, a plastic material which can be chemically altered for rigidity or flexibility dependent on the application, and which has become the go-to material for quality aftermarket suspension bushes for both restoration and modification. Unlike rubber, polyurethane is not affected by oil or petrol, making it perfectly suited for use beneath a classic, where oil leaks are somewhat inevitable.

Polyurethane bushes are available for the Minor from a number of suppliers at a variety of price points. The

The Minor's suspension can be tweaked to eliminate wallowing and produce a very nicely handling car indeed.

Modern rubber bushes (foreground), in the author's experience, tend to deteriorate at an alarming rate. Polyurethane (background), then, is the way to go.

Polyurethane bush kits for the Minor are available at a range of price points, from a number of suppliers and manufacturers, and with differing shore ratings. Consider your requirements and budget.

Use polyurethane bush grease if supplied with your kit, or petroleum jelly to lubricate the bushes for installation.

Fitting polyurethane bushes to your Minor should be achievable within a weekend for any competent home mechanic.

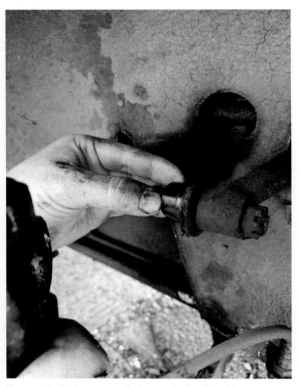

Top trunnion bushes are usually the most badly affected by wear, as they take the most hammer over bumps and potholes.

cheapest polyurethane bushes, available from most specialist Minor part suppliers for less than £40 for a full car set at the time of writing, last well; however, they tend to be somewhat harder than the standard rubber bushes they replace. This is not a problem in terms of performance, as a harder bush gives better location of the suspension components it interfaces with, but these bushes do give a harsher than standard ride and transmit more noise through to the cabin, due to a reduction in compressibility and therefore the insulating properties previously mentioned.

Tie rod bushes prevent the lower wishbone moving forward under braking. The easiest method of fitting new bushes, in the author's experience, is to leave the tie rod disconnected until the front nut has been engaged in its threads, before refitting the wishbone end.

Note that although polyurethane bushes have a longer service life than rubber items, they are not entirely 'fit and forget'.

Softer 'comfort'-grade polyurethane bushes are available from specialist suppliers such as Polybush, who offer bushes with a range of shore ratings, comfort being the most compliant through dynamic to the harshest performance grade, which is ideal for fast road and track use. These are a more expensive option – £135 at time of writing for a full set from www.polybush.co.uk – but the comfort-grade bushes claim to offer the compressability of the OE rubber bushes without the short lifespan of modern aftermarket replacement rubber items, a claim which the bushes stand up to in the author's experience.

Striking a balance between performance and comfort is key to enjoying your Minor to the maximum. The harder the bush, the more noise and vibration from the road wheels and suspension will be passed through into the cabin, but for fast road or track use, the pay-off of sharper steering and reduced body roll due to the compressibility of the bushes may be worth the compromise. Do not underestimate the importance of this insulation from the road when it comes to driver and passenger comfort, though, and consider your car's intended use carefully before deciding which bush hardness you desire.

Replacing your Minor's suspension bushes is a time-consuming task, but well-worth doing as a fresh set of bushes, whatever material or grade you choose, will transform the handling and ride of your Minor compared to soggy originals. The task should be within the reach of any competent home mechanic, with the biggest challenge that you are likely to face being releasing corroded fixings. Before embarking on the task, however, it is worth ensuring that you have all of the relevant tools and components handy – unless you are blessed with the space for the car to sit in pieces while additional components are ordered should the need arise. It is also advisable to soak all of the fixings that you will need to disturb, along with the splines of the torsion bar where it enters the lower wishbone, with a quality penetrating fluid in the days prior to you tackling this task – you will be glad you did!

LOWERING THE RIDE HEIGHT

Altering the ride height is one of the most common suspension modifications, and is one which can be done without any financial outlay, so long as the suspension is fundamentally in fine fettle. Although a slightly lowered car can be better in the bends, owing to a lower centre of gravity and reduced suspension travel – particularly if the lower ride height is teamed with the addition of stiffer springs at the rear and an anti roll bar up front – the main aim of most owners who drop their Minor by an inch or two is to to allow the wheels, aesthetically, to fill the arches better. As such, it is worth thinking about your wheel and tyre choices first. 13-inch wheels, for example, will never fill the arches unless the suspension is dropped dangerously low (*see* note below), whereas if 15-inch wheels are fitted, or even 14s with a tall tyre sidewall profile, consideration must be given to clearance between the top of the tyre and the wheel arch when the steering is at full lock. Also consider the implications of bumping up a curb at full lock, as this will cause the suspension to compress where clearance between top of tyre and bottom of wheel arch is already tight.

> **A note of caution: how low is too low?**
> Lowering the ride height of the Minor too much will have a dangerously adverse effect on the handling. Under bump, it is possible for the steering arms to bottom out on the inner wings, locking or jarring the steering. It is the purpose of the rubber bump stops to prevent this happening under normal use. If the bump stops are to be cut to allow increased suspension travel once the ride height has been lowered, it is essential that sufficient length is left so that the rubber stop is hit and any compression is taken up before the steering arms make contact with the bodywork.

Front Height Adjustment

Dropping the ride height at the front is a fairly straightforward process which can be achieved within a few hours. Having said that, it pays to bear in mind that those few hours could be spent fighting with just one seized fixing, so be sure to spend some time applying penetrating fluid to the fasteners and torsion bar splines where they enter the lower arm a few days before tackling the job at hand.

Finer adjustment can be made by altering the position of the rear mounting point of the torsion bar, via the Vernier plates at their rear where they mount to the crossmember. This fine adjustment is usually used to adjust side-to-side discrepancy rather than to lower the car. Lowering (or, indeed, raising) the ride height of the car is done simply by moving the position of the lower suspension arm on the splines of the torsion bar. Each spline equates to roughly 1½ inches of movement.

Let us take you through this process step-by-step. On our guinea pig car, the author's own Morris Minor saloon, we are raising the ride height by one spline, as the car's ride height had been set too low and the steering arms were bottoming out on the inner wings on bumps or under heavy braking. However, the process for adjusting the ride height is the same no matter if you are lowering or raising the ride height, with only the direction of movement of the lower arm on the splines of the torsion bar stating whether the car will be raised or dropped.

Tools list:
AF spanners
Socket set
Soft-faced hammer
Correction fluid or white paint pen
Trolley jack
Axle stands

1) Loosen the wheel nuts ¼ turn each with the car on the floor and the handbrake on, then raise the car and position on axle stands under the chassis legs.
2) Remove the road wheels and carefully mark using correction fluid or a paint marker from the suspension bottom arm to the torsion bar to act as a reference for its current position.
3) Use a trolley jack on the rearmost half of the lower arm to load the torsion bar slightly, which will allow it to be dismantled.

DANGER: Ensure you have the lower arm well supported on the jack and do not place any part of your body beneath the arm when it is raised in this way. If it slips from the jack, or the jack fails, the arm will be pushed downwards with force and could cause serious injury.

4) Remove the vertical $\frac{5}{16}$ UNF (½ AF spanner size) bolt which retains the tie rod (this prevents the hub moving forward in the arch under braking) and tuck the tie rod beneath the lower arm, then remove the bracket (¾ AF spanner size) in which the tie rod sat, which

reassembly. (Total 4 x $\frac{3}{8}$ spring washers per side + 1 x $\frac{5}{16}$ spring washer. Make sure you have these in stock before embarking on the job).

6) Remove the $\frac{9}{16}$ AF spanner size bolt that secures the two halves of the lower arm together from the inner end of the arm. If this has a nyloc nut fitted, replace this nut on re-assembly ($\frac{3}{8}$ UNF).

7) Remove the $\frac{9}{16}$ spanner size nut and spring washer from the end of the torsion bar and carefully remove the front half of the lower arm.

8) Carefully remove the threaded portion of the lower trunnion from the rearmost half of the lower arm. Ensuring that the flexible brake hose is not stressed, prop the king pin assembly clear of the lower arm. A piece of wood between the backplate to kingpin bolts and the inner wheel arch works well.

9) Lower the jack to release tension on the torsion bar. Noting the mark you made earlier, use a soft-faced hammer to drift the lower arm backwards along the torsion bar splines until it comes free. It may be corroded and stiff, and may require heat/penetrating oil to start it moving. Once the lower arm is clear of the splines, take the opportunity to clean the spines with a wire brush and apply a smear of copper grease to prevent future corrosion and aid future disassembly.

10) Locate the lower arm of the splines of the torsion bar in the new desired position. Each spline equates to roughly 1½ inches difference in ride height. To lower the car, the arm must be replaced with its outer end higher than it was removed. If the ride height is to be raised, it must be lower. A torsion bar is essentially an unwound spring. To lower the car, the spring needs to be de-tensioned, hence the arm comes up. Use a

doubles as one of the fixings that secures the two halves of the lower arm together.

5) Remove the two $\frac{9}{16}$ AF spanner size nuts and spring washers from either side of the lower trunnion. Replace these, and all other sporting washers on

drop after it has been at full droop. Check clearance between the bump stops and the top trunnion. Re-check fasteners for tightness after a few miles.

Rear Ride Height Adjustment

To lower the back of the car, lowering blocks can be used between the axle and springs to raise the relative position of the hub centre in the wheel arch. Aluminium lowering blocks are placed between the axle and spring, with longer than standard U-bolts used to secure the axle to the spring. Depending on the amount lowered and the condition of the springs, it may be necessary to shorten the height of the rubber bump stops that sit atop the axle. In order to retain some level of compressibility once the tapered cone element of the bump stop is removed, the cut bump stops can be cross drilled.

> **A note of caution: have your springs sprung?**
> Before lowering the car, it is a good idea to assess the condition of the leaf springs and bushes, and take the opportunity to rectify any issues first. Reproduction leaf springs have a tendency to flatten over time, far faster than original springs. To counter this, many owners opt to fit stiffer, 7-leaf, Minor Traveller springs to saloons which would have been fitted with 5-leaf springs from standard.

soft-faced hammer to drive the lower arm back along the spline from whence it came. Check your mark to ensure you have moved the intended number of splines.

11) Re-assembly is pretty much the reverse as disassembly. First, raise the outer end of the lower wishbone to load the torsion bar then refit the rearmost side of the lower trunnion with its nut and a new spring washer.

12) Offer up the front half of the lower arm and use the $\frac{3}{8}$ UNF securing bolt to pull them tightly together, then replace the nuts on the front of the lower trunnion and the end of the torsion bar with new spring washers and tighten fully.

13) Refit the tie rod bracket loosely, then fit the tie rod with its $\frac{5}{16}$ UNF vertical bolt. Finally tighten the bracket nut. Re-check all fasteners for tightness, then replace the road wheel. Repeat the process on the other side.

14) Bounce or take the car for a short drive to settle the suspension before making any further adjustments. You will be surprised how much the suspension will

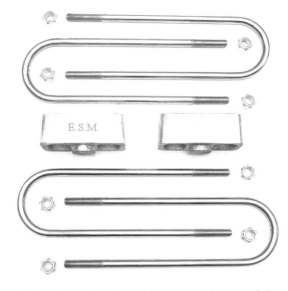

Lowering kits which include extended U-bolts as well as a pair of alloy lowering blocks are available in both 1.25- and 1.75-inch thicknesses.

Shopping list:
4x Extended U bolts with 8x nyloc nuts
2x Lowering blocks
4x Spring pad bushes as required
4x Pressed steel spring pad retaining plates as required
2x Bump stops as required

Tool list:
Trolley jack
Axle stands
$\frac{9}{16}$ UNF socket/ratchet or spanner. (**Note:** some cars use $\frac{5}{8}$ AF fixings)
Hammer

1) Raise the car and support the body on axle stands. Support under the rear spring hangers and/or boot floor, using a block of wood to spread the load on the latter. Allow the axle to droop fully.
2) Undo the four nyloc nuts (or eight flat nuts) from the over-axle U bolts on one side. Remove the U bolts and rubber bump stop which they retain. Allow the under-spring damper brackets to drop away with their dampers still attached.

6) Now repeat the process on the other side. You will need to re-check the U bolt nuts for tightness after a few miles to ensure that they have not become loose as the spring pads have compressed.

ANTI-ROLL BAR

Simple, bolt-on, front anti-roll bar kits are readily available for the Morris Minor and can be used to prevent body roll and produce sharper turn-in when cornering. The bar joins the lower arms of the suspension, acting in essence as a third torsion bar across the front of the car.

In the accompanying images, we are fitting an anti-roll bar kit from ESM Morris Minors (part number SUS200), which comes supplied with detailed instructions so what follows is merely an overview of the process. The ARB is secured to the chassis in a pair of bushings, the brackets for which are bolted to the chassis legs, and to the suspension via the tie bar yoke.

Although the kits are sold as bolt-on, with the transverse ARB support bolted through the chassis legs, they can also be welded for a stronger, albeit more permanent, mounting. Note, however, that the front mounting bracket positions may need to be altered if the ride height is to be adjusted – a task made much more difficult if the bracket has been welded to the chassis leg. If it is your desire to weld the mounting bracket to the chassis leg,

3) Use a jack to raise the axle by a few inches. Ensure that the spring pad bush and its pressed steel plate remain on top of the spring. Inspect the condition of the axle spring pads that sit either side of the road spring and replace if less than perfect. Consider upgrading to polyurethane versions at this stage (*see* previous information).

4) Insert lowering blocks between the spring and the axle, nipple up, ensuring that the spring pads and the metal locating plates are in position. Lower the axle onto the lowering blocks, ensuring that the lowering block is located in the hole on the axle mounting bracket and on the peg of the pressed steel bush plate. Replace the bump stop on top of the axle and the damper bracket below the axle in the same positions from which they were removed.

5) Thread the replacement, longer, U bolts through the stack just as they were removed and fit fresh nyloc nuts on the bottom, tightening progressively to ensure the axle is firmly secured.

An anti-roll bar is a straightforward bolt-on modification which can transform the handling of your Minor.

the author suggests installing the ARB as a bolt-on kit for an initial trial period, with adjustment possible by slotting the hole in the chassis leg, and only welding the bracket in position after a few months of testing and when you are sure that the ride height does not need to be altered.

Tools required:
Trolley jack
Axle stands
½-in AF socket/ratchet and spanner
Screwdriver/lever
Parallel punch set
Red rubber grease or petroleum jelly (the latter not to be used on rubber bushes)
Drill with ⁵⁄₁₆ in/8mm bit
Allen key to suit bush clamping bolt

Fit an Anti-roll Bar

1) Raise the front of the car and place axle stands under the front chassis legs. Using petroleum jelly (poly) or red rubber grease (rubber) to lubricate the bushes, push the end attachments onto each end of the anti-roll bar to about halfway up the tapered spigot.

2) Attach the front bushes and mounting brackets and lay the roll bar in position beneath the car. Note that the mounting brackets may be fitted either on the inside or outside of the chassis leg, depending on your installation. Remove the vertical tie bar bolts from each side of the car and, supporting the ARB on a trolley jack at the front, raise it into position, and insert the threaded pins on the end pieces in place of the tie rod bolts. Loosely fit their securing nut.

3) Adjust the position of the roll bar so that the front brackets sit just forward of the tie bar mounts on the chassis legs. Reposition the axle stands under the lower suspension arm so that the car's weight is compressing the suspension. Alternatively, this may be done with the car resting on the ground, so long as there is sufficient clearance to drill the chassis leg (next step) or on drive-on ramps.

4) Use a trolley jack to raise each mounting bracket in turn firmly against the chassis leg and drill horizontally through the chassis to secure the bracket. Note that large alterations in ride height may necessitate moving the position of this bracket if the geometry changes cannot be accounted for by means of sliding the ends of the bar fore/aft through the end attachments.

5) Install the supplied bolts through the chassis leg to secure the front mounting brackets, then tighten all the fixings. Re-check all fasteners for tightness after a test drive.

TELESCOPIC DAMPERS

From the factory, Minors were fitted with Armstrong lever arm shock absorbers (dampers) front and rear. At the front, these also double as the top suspension mounting pivot, whereas at the rear they are simply bolted onto a bracket below the centre of the spring under the axle with a drop link connected to a peg on the body.

Lever arm shock absorbers have a tendency to overheat or suffer from oil cavitation (foaming) under heavy use, so

Telescopic front damper kits are available as oil-filled, gas-filled, adjustable, or coil-assisted.

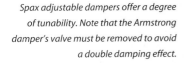

Spax adjustable dampers offer a degree of tunability. Note that the Armstrong damper's valve must be removed to avoid a double damping effect.

if your desired driving style necessitates lots of load on the suspension, telescopic shock absorbers are certainly an upgrade worth pursuing. Several kits at a variety of price points are available from oil-damped through gas-damped to coil-assisted telescopic dampers known colloquially as 'coil overs'.

Front telescopic dampers are, in almost all cases, mounted via brackets that protrude through the inner wing, which must be cut to allow this, and pick up on the original lever arm damper, which is retained as a top pivot. The valve in the lever arm damper must be removed to prevent a double damping effect and prolong the life of the unit as a pivot. The lever arm damper should be refilled with oil of the correct grade after the valve has been removed to ensure its bearings are adequately lubricated and prevent collapse and failure. Bottom mounting assemblies are fixed to the lower wishbone.

On the rear, the original lever arm dampers can be removed completely along with their under-spring mounting bracket (*see* advice on lowering the rear earlier in this chapter, where the process of safely lifting the axle away from the rear spring is described). A replacement

Coil-assisted dampers offer a great deal of adjustability, and firm up the front spring rate – especially useful on a lowered car with an unwound torsion bar.

Most rear telescopic damper kits are supplied with a bolt- or weld-on cross-member for the top mounting. Fitting is a straightforward enough job.

Some owners use the original lever arm drop link mounting pin as a top mount.

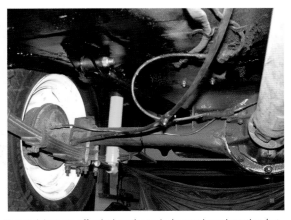

Turreted dampers offer the best theoretical mounting orientation, but require the boot floor to be cut and mounts welded in.

under-spring bracket (included in the kit with the dampers) should be fitted in place of the original and, at the top, a cross-member fitted and bolted through the boot floor. (**Note:** You will need to remove the boot floor panels and spare wheel to gain access for this.) The telescopic dampers can then be fitted between these points. Note that this simple bolt-on kit offers a great improvement over the original dampers, particularly if these are worn and at the end of their useful service life; however, the necessary inward angle of the dampers is not optimum. JLH Morris Minors offers a kit, and fitting service, for turreted rear dampers that require a suspension turret to be welded into the boot space. This allows the damper to work in a more optimal vertical plane; however, the significant cost, cutting and welding involved means that this is not a commonly adopted option for most road cars.

Coil-assisted telescopic dampers (often referred to as 'coil overs') are particularly beneficial for significantly lowered cars, and use an assister spring to complement the Minor's original torsion bar and leaf spring set-up. A torsion bar is essentially an uncoiled spring, and its spring rate is softened the lower the car's ride height is set, as tension is removed from the spring.

Coil over damper kits mount in much the same way as the telescopic dampers described above, but use stronger mounts. The advantages of coil over dampers are an increased spring rate without the need for upgraded torsion bars (front) or leaf springs (at the rear) as well as enhanced adjustability of ride height by compressing or relaxing the assister spring.

REAR SPRINGS

Late Minor saloons were originally fitted with five-leaf rear springs (i.e. a stack of five lengths of hardened and tempered spring steel making up the spring). Early cars used seven thinner leaves to give the same spring rate.

If eight-leaf springs are to be fitted, four hybrid bushes (ESM part number SUS727A) are required.

These low-strength, seven-leaf springs are no longer available new and therefore if restoring an early car to standard specification, five-leaf aftermarket replacements must be fitted unless the expensive option of having original springs reconditioned or a custom set of springs made is to be explored.

Over time, springs lose their temper and also wear on their rubbing surfaces. Refurbishing a set of slightly worn springs is possible by carefully deconstructing and cleaning them, linishing any wear 'steps' with an angle grinder and re-stacking them with thick grease applied between each leaf. However, if the springs have lost their temper (springiness), they must either be professionally reconditioned or replaced entirely.

If your Minor is lowered, and/or the front suspension has been fitted with thicker torsion bars or an anti-roll bar, it pays to increase the rear spring rate to redress this balance. Travellers were originally fitted with seven-leaf

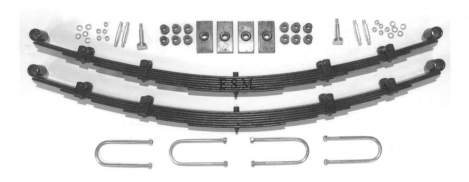

Complete spring fitting kits are available with both polyurethane and rubber bushes and a choice of five (saloon), seven (Traveller) and eight (LCV) leaf springs.

springs, owing to their larger loadbay, allowing them to carry four adults plus a load of 100lb, or a driver plus 5cwt, and therefore these springs make a simple like-for-like off the shelf swap to increase the rear spring rate, just requiring longer Traveller U bolts to be used.

Vans and pickups were fitted with 8-leaf springs, but use a different size eye bush and therefore, until recently, were not interchangeable for saloon/travellers. A new (at time of writing) hybrid bush is now available (ESM part number SUS727A) to allow the fitting of these larger-shackle sized springs to a saloon, convertible or traveller. These springs may be useful if very heavy payloads are to be carried or if your Minor is to be used for towing regularly.

The JLH coil over damper kit does away with the torsion bar set-up entirely but is far from a bolt-on solution.

Five-link rear suspension kit requires careful setting up by a skilled engineer.

Getting the spring rates perfect on your Minor in the pursuit of optimal balance may take a little trial and error, and will depend on loads and number of occupants you are likely to be carrying on a regular basis as well as weight distribution changes from other modifications. Custom spring sets may be created by adding or subtracting leaves from a spring stack, with many owners opting for six-leaf hybrid spring sets for a good balance between compliance and road holding on saloons.

GOING FURTHER...

Having covered variations on the BMC theme, we will now explore some more extreme suspension modifications which are available as off-the-shelf kits to improve the handling characteristics of your Minor.

JLH Morris Minors offers a coil over damper kit for the front of the Minor that dispenses with the torsion bar completely alongside a 5-link rear suspension kit which does away with the leaf springs. Aimed at the fast road and track use market, both modifications must be tackled by a competent engineer, and will require setting-up carefully to ensure that the safety of your Minor on the road is not compromised by poor suspension geometry. However, if fitted and set up correctly, the benefits are unarguably superb handling. Indeed, the five-leaf rear suspension set-up is sold only to be fitted in house by the kits' manufacturer to ensure that it is set up correctly.

Modifications for the rear suspension also available from JLH include a turreted rear shock absorber conversion that allows the telescopic damper to work at its optimum angle. However, this requires the boot floor to be cut and a new suspension turret welded in place for the damper top mount, as well as a rear radius arm kit which is designed to prevent axle tramp associated with fitting higher power engines to a Minor with standard rear suspension. Again, welding and specialist set-up is required for this modification.

If much more power than standard is to be transmitted through the rear axle, upgrading to a stronger axle from a more powerful car may be required. Common swaps are to Ford Escort MkII axles (100-mm PCD – *see* Chapter 8) or Triumph Dolomite Sprint axles (3.75-inch PCD). JLH is able to supply a fitting kit for the former axle.

12

Electrics

Before working on any electrical circuit, disconnect the battery to prevent the risk of a short circuit. Always remove the earth terminal first, and replace it last, to avoid the risk of a short between the live terminal clamp and the body of the car via a spanner being used to slacken the clamp.

Before embarking on any electrical system upgrades, it is important to establish that your Minor's electrical system is in good health (*see* Chapter 4). With this established we can be sure that we are upgrading for a genuine benefit, and not introducing additional loads into an already ailing electrical system.

The Minor's electrical circuits, from standard, are not particularly well protected, with sidelights (until 1962) and headlights (all models) unfused. As such, care should always be taken to avoid short circuits.

Brand new wiring looms are available for all years of Morris Minor, either to OE specification held in stock by numerous Morris Minor parts suppliers or to order direct from manufacturers Autosparks (www.autosparks.co.uk), who offer bespoke additions to the standard loom to suit your electrical needs. The latter enables a very neat, tidy and safe installation and is well worth considering if your original loom is tired and you are planning a number of electrical modifications to your Minor.

ISOLATOR SWITCH

Fitting a battery cut-off switch to your Minor is one of the simplest beneficial modifications that can be undertaken. Most commonly connected between a battery earth terminal and the bodywork of the car, they allow electrical isolation without the need to physically disconnect the battery terminal. (Fitting a cut-out on the earth side of the circuit minimises the number of 'hot' battery terminals available under the bonnet; however, in some instances the isolator is fitted on the live circuit and terminals protected with rubber boots.) This is useful for security (if the isolator is hidden, or its key removed) and electrical safety. In the event of a short-circuit, which could rapidly lead to damage and even a fire, the electrical system can be isolated easily. Similarly, if work is to be undertaken on the electrical system, a battery isolator allows power to be dis-

connected without the need to physically remove the battery earth terminal. A fully isolated battery in storage also prevents low amperage draws from items with keep-alive memories such as aftermarket radios, clocks, etc., draining the battery over a prolonged lay-up.

Various types of isolator switch are available, each with their own pros and cons. The ubiquitous 'Red Key' type remains the most common choice, and can be mounted through the bulkhead so that the battery can be isolated from within the cabin. This is especially useful firstly as a security device, as the red key can be removed and stored away from the car, but also enables power to be cut from the electrical circuits in the event of an accident or short-circuit to prevent a fire.

Fixed key switches can be fitted in the same way, but as the name suggests, the key cannot be removed as a security measure. It cannot be lost either, so consider your own fallibility before making your decision, and note that spare red keys can be purchased for a modest cost and are well worth keeping somewhere safe in case aforementioned fallibility is demonstrated…

Screw-type isolators, eg. Dis-Carnect offer an incredibly simple method of fitment and are ideal if you simply wish to disconnect the battery for long-term storage or maintenance. The disadvantage, of course, is that the bonnet must be raised for isolation and reconnection. Remote-type isolators are available that fit in much the

Red key isolator is a popular upgrade.

Screw-type isolators are simple to install and are ideal for disconnecting the battery while the car is in storage, but less accessible than an isolator within the cabin.

same way as the Dis-Carnect device, and are worth considering if you wish to be able to isolate the battery without raising the bonnet but do not wish to drill into the bodywork or alter the battery cables in any way. However, these are a more expensive option.

The simplest method of fitting an isolator is to install the terminal type. To fit a key-type isolator, fixed or removable, involves drilling three holes in your Minor's bulkhead, so this is not one for purists or advocates of purely bolt-on modifications. However, it is a very convenient method of keeping high amperage cables within the engine bay while allowing the battery to be isolated from within the cabin. The first hole should be drilled large enough

to provide clearance for the isolator 'nose' to protrude through the bulkhead and into the cabin somewhere accessible in the passenger (for right-hand drive cars) footwell, adjacent to the battery earth. The simplest and cheapest method for drilling such a hole is by means of a step drill. Alternatively, a Q-max type punch cutter may be used and will produce a cleaner hole. With the switch placed in position, two holes for securing bolts may be marked, drilled and securing bolts fitted, either via rivet nuts or a nut and bolt through the bulkhead.

The electrical side of the installation is simplicity itself. An insulated earth lead from the battery clamp must replace the original bare cable, and this is joined between the battery earth and one side of the switch. The other side of the switch should be wired to the car body earth point.

A fused bypass from the battery side of either switch type's battery earth terminal to ground may be fitted to allow radio memory or any aftermarket clocks, etc., to continue to be powered even when the battery is disconnected. However, the fuse will blow immediately if an attempt is made to start the car without the main connection being re-made (the fuse rating must be low enough that it will blow when the ignition is turned on to prevent the possibility of the car being bump started). Clearly a fused bypass as described above continues to offer the security advantage; however, it does not protect the battery from being drained by these devices during a prolonged lay-up.

If you choose to fit the isolator to the live side of the battery, it should be positioned between the battery and the starter solenoid. In this instance, the live feed originally wired to the solenoid should be connected to one side of the isolator and a new cable fitted between the isolator and solenoid. The isolator's wiring must in this instance be insulated with rubber boots to prevent the risk of a short-circuit.

POSITIVE TO NEGATIVE EARTH CONVERSION

From the factory, all Morris Minors were wired positive earth. This means that the positive terminal of the battery is connected to the body of the car (on a Minor, this is via a cable to the fuel pump side of the battery box), and the negative terminal of the battery is connected to the starter solenoid, which acts as a junction box to feed all of the car's electrical components.

By now, most Minors have been converted to negative earth, in line with more modern electrical systems that allow the simple fitment of aftermarket accessories such as modern radios and other in-car entertainment options (*see* Chapter 14), 12-volt sockets, electronic ignition modules and modern alternators.

In a positive earth system, electrons flow from the negative side of the battery through components and to a positive ground. Today, convention dictates that all cars are wired negative earth, with that electron flow reversed. The reasons behind this change are unclear, with electrolytic corrosion being a greater problem for positive earth cars one theory, and simple convention due to a requirement to use shared components another. Either way, negative earth electrical systems became the norm not long after the Minor left production and today it makes sense to change the polarity of your Minor's electrical system to fit with that convention, allowing the straightforward fitment of any of the electrical upgrades which will be detailed later in this chapter.

The process of changing from positive to negative earth is straightforward. Those without aftermarket alterations or factory option alternators and dealer-fit radios are the most straightforward to convert. The starter, windscreen wiper and heater motors will continue to work normally, as will the ignition system (although the coil wiring should be switched for efficiency), lights, fuel pump (original points type – electronic aftermarket pumps are polarity-sensitive and will need to be changed), aftermarket heated screens, etc., so reversing the polarity is relatively simple, only the dynamo requiring a simple re-polarisation for it to work correctly. But for the avoidance of doubt, we will walk you through the process below:

1) Ascertain the existing polarity

If your Minor is up and running with a battery fitted, it requires only a glance at the polarity markings to determine which of the battery's terminals is connected to the car's bodywork. If, however, you have acquired your Minor as a project, it may be slightly trickier to ascertain. Positive battery terminals are larger than negative terminals and this is reflected by the size of the battery clamps. Negative terminals are 17.5mm measured at the largest end of the cone, and positive terminals are 19.5mm. If the terminals measure 13.1mm and 14.7mm respectively, a previous owner has fitted a Japanese battery, which has smaller terminals. If you have a car that has been in storage for a long time, you may even find someone had fitted flag terminals, as fitted to Fords of the day. If battery cables are fitted, check for a + or – marking on the earth side cable. If not, check the coil connections. Although the

car will still run if the coil has not had its wires swapped (and therefore this could be a red herring), for reliable running, the coil's power feed requires switching for negative earth conversion (more on this later). If the earth wire (white with a black tracer) that connects the low tension side of the coil to the distributor is connected to the – (or SW) terminal on the coil, the coil is wired negative earth and has likely already been converted. It won't hurt, however, to follow the next steps in any case to ensure success.

2) Battery terminals

If you have established that your Minor is currently wired positive earth and wish to change its polarity to negative earth, the first step is to disconnect the battery terminals from the battery. As discussed in this chapter introduction, always disconnect the earth terminal first and on refitting, reconnect it last to avoid a short-circuit if your spanner happens to touch the body when tightening the final terminal. Remove the battery fully to aid access and prevent the risk of a short-circuit while working in the battery box. As mentioned in the previous step, positive terminals are larger than negative terminals and as such, the battery terminals will need to be swapped side to side or replaced. Depending on the type of battery clamps fitted to your Minor, you may simply be able to disconnect them from the heavy wires and swap them over for one another. If your Minor features cast, soldered or crimp-type terminals, however, you will either need to make new leads or simply purchase a replacement pre-made set either from your local motor factor (using your original cables as guides for the lengths required) or from a Morris Minor specialist parts supplier. Note that the thickness and therefore current-carrying ability of the battery cables is the most important criterion, and it is therefore worth erring on the side of bigger-section cables than thinner, especially if the engine has been, or is to be, tuned with a higher compression ratio, etc. Battery cables also degrade over time, so if they are looking a little tired, now is as good a time as any to renew them for new. When replacing the earth cable, ensure it is making good, clean contact with the car's bodywork, which should have been cleaned back to bare, shiny steel, then protected with silicone/dielectric grease to prevent corrosion. The terminals, too, should be cleaned of oxidation and protected in a similar manner. Replace the setscrew as well for maximum conduction. Loose connections or those to painted or corroded surfaces will risk a poor connection and result in electrical faults. Once the cables are swapped, you may replace the battery and connect the live now positive (+) terminal; however, do not reconnect the earth now negative (–) terminal until the process is complete.

3) Coil

Although the car will run without altering wiring to the coil, to work correctly and efficiently, the coil's polarity must be swapped so that the negative (–) terminal (sometimes marked CB (Contact Breaker)) is connected to the terminal on the side of the distributor. The wire for this should be white with a black tracer line along its length. The positive (+) terminal of the coil (sometimes marked SW (Switch)) must now be fed by the ignition live (positive) feed from the ignition switch. This wire should be plain white. As previously mentioned, the car will run without this wire swap, as the coil is an alternating current device; however, swapping the wires ensures that a negative HT spark is fed to the plugs – electrons prefer to jump from hot surfaces to colder surfaces, ideally from the centre electrode to the earth electrode, therefore swapping polarity aids combustion.

Note: We are assuming here that the car is still using a points and condenser ignition system. However, if your car is fitted with a positive earth electronic ignition module, this must be removed and replaced with a negative earth version, which are more common and readily available (*see* Chapter 5).

4) Fuel pump

A standard points-type SU fuel pump will work without any modification no matter the polarity; however, modern electronic replacements are polarity sensitive. These are earthed through their body and so if you have a car fitted with a positive-earth electronic pump, it must be replaced with a negative-earth version, or a points-type pump.

5) Dynamo

Although the dynamo wiring does not require changing, the dynamo will need to be polarised so that it charges the battery correctly. To do this, disconnect both the large (D) and small (F) terminals and with the battery connected, run a wire from the positive terminal of the battery and brush it two or three times against the F terminal until a small blue spark is seen. The D and F wires can now be replaced and the dynamo is ready for use with the negative earth system. Once the conversion is complete, test that it charges correctly, first by ensuring that the red 'ignition' no charge warning light illuminates with the ignition on and extinguishes once the engine is started, but double-check by connecting a multimeter across the battery on the 20V DC scale. An increase in voltage (to around 13.5 volts) should be observed with the engine running and revs increased to around 2,000 rpm.

Note: If your Minor has a positive earth alternator fitted (as fitted from factory to some late Travellers, as well as special-option vehicles such as police cars), this will need to be replaced with a negative earth unit. Similarly, if you have replaced your dynamo regulator with an electronic unit wired for positive earth, this will need replacing for a negative earth version. An original points-operated regulator unit will work irrespective of the polarity change.

6) Aftermarket accessories

One of the biggest benefits of changing the polarity of your Minor to negative earth is the world of opportunities it opens up for aftermarket accessories. However, if your previously positive-earth Minor had accessories fitted prior to the conversion, it pays to check that they are either not polarity-sensitive or that their wiring can be altered so that they work with the negative earth system. The most common accessory you are likely to find is a car radio and possibly an electronic clock. Many older radios will have a polarity switch on the back which can be changed from positive to negative earth. If a negative earth radio has been fitted on an insulated base and wired to work with the positive earth set-up, this will need to be reset to its original specification by earthing the body and connecting to a positive feed. An electronic clock wired up incorrectly will invariably damage it irreparably, so replace it with another clock with negative earth. 12-volt accessory sockets should be wired so that the outside of the socket is negative, the pin at the base of the socket, positive. Again, if such sockets have been insulated and wired while the car was still positive earth, these will need rewiring to ensure that they remain compatible with accessories such as phone chargers and satellite navigation systems which rely on them. Other aftermarket accessories should be taken on a case-by-case basis. Generally if there are two wires (a live and an earth) going into an accessory, its polarity can be reversed by simply switching these wires. If only a live feed enters a positive earth accessory and it takes its earth from its casing, then it may need either insulating from ground and wiring accordingly or ideally swapping for a negative earth equivalent.

ALTERNATOR UPGRADE

Use of the Minor's standard dynamo is a relatively inefficient way of charging the battery, and so if accessories are to be added and/or regular use is intended, where wipers, heater and light are all likely to be in use at the same time, upgrading to an alternator is a must. Even BMC upgraded to alternators on Morris Minors in the final year of Traveller production at Adderley Park, and 11AC alternators were fitted, alongside specially calibrated speedometers, to some Morris Minor police cars.

In short, an alternator is a more efficient way of charging the battery than the original dynamo. An alternator charges at idle, whereas a dynamo does not, and is likely to be internally regulated, too, meaning that the regula-

tor box on the bulkhead can either be dispensed with altogether or used simply as a junction box. In fact, there are even dummy regulators on the market that simply include a bridging piece, or in some cases a 40 amp fuse, to join together wires to positions A1, A2 and A3 with wire D. These dummy regulators are often used in conjunction with 'Dynamator' or 'dynalite' alternator conversions, which give the appearance of a dynamo with all of the advantages of an alternator. These are a great way of converting to an alternator without changing the under-bonnet aesthetic of your Morris Minor. We will look at these in more detail later on.

Until recently, one of the main disadvantages of converting to an alternator was the loss of the coil's mounting on the dynamo and the need to relocate it, requiring the drilling of holes in bodywork – which went against the ethos of 'bolt on, bolt off' modifications prized my many owners. Help is now at hand thanks to a nifty redesign to the alternator rear mounting bracket, which allows the coil to be fixed in its original position above the new alternator with ease. This redesigned bracket does not come as standard in some kits, so be aware of what you are ordering if this is the option you are looking for.

Alternator conversion kits that include all physical and electrical mounting hardware are available from all of

Alternator conversion kits are available, which include the bracketry, fan belt and sub-loom as well as instructions required for the conversion.

Spending the extra on the alternator mounting bracket which incorporates the coil mounting (ESM part number ALT104A) is well worthwhile.

the main Morris Minor parts suppliers and fitting them is straightforward. A wiring sub-loom and connector plug that fits directly to the rear of the alternator is provided with most kits, along with wiring diagrams and fitting instructions. Note that these aftermarket alternators are almost invariably designed for negative earth applications.

Alternator Alternatives

If you would prefer to preserve the original under-bonnet look of your Minor but would still like to improve upon the original charging system, there are a couple of alternatives options available to you.

Alternator concealed in a dynamo housing makes the upgrade invisible.

First up are the various cleverly disguised alternators within dynamo casings which promise modern charging performance in a discreet package. These are particularly desirable to owners wishing to use their Minor in all weathers (using the heater, lights and wipers all together will often result in electrical demand outstripping dynamo supply), without altering the under-bonnet appearance of their car.

Also worth considering is keeping the original dynamo, or having it rewound and rebuilt to a standard as good as new, but doing away with the often troublesome Lucas voltage regulator cut-out. These points-based devices are famously difficult to set up and the contact points can corrode and stick, causing either over- or under-charging after periods of storage. Classic Dynamo and Regulator Conversions Ltd in Lincolnshire offer a fully electronic regulator concealed within an original housing as a plug-and-play alternative to the troublesome original units. So discreet are these units that they are even approved for use by the famously fastidious Vintage Sports Car Club for use on competitive vintage vehicles.

ELECTRIC COOLING FAN

The Minor's standard metal cooling fan bolts to the front of the water pump and thrashes around at all times when the engine is running. At high engine revs, it spins quickly; at low revs, such as when idling in traffic when it is most needed, it does not. It is not a particularly efficient design, and serves also to produce unnecessary noise, sap power as the engine fights to push it through the air and runs continuously, even when it is not needed. One

An electric fan can be mounted on the engine side of the radiator or…

Thermostatically controlled fan switches come in many guises. This offering from Revotec fits into the bottom hose…

…just behind the grille, depending on other packaging constraints.

last problem is that the fan will not clear the timing cover canister-type breather fitted to 1275 engines, which must be modified to a 'D'-top profile if the original fan is to be used. Removing these in favour of an unbreathed Minor front plate is not an option, as the engine will leak oil due to excess crankcase pressure.

A thermostatically – or manual switch – controlled electric fan, then, is a sensible upgrade for any Minor and is near-essential if a larger capacity engine is to be fitted. Companies such as Revotec Ltd (www.revotec.com) can supply either a kit of parts specifically designed for the Minor or individual components, allowing you to source the best-quality and best-suited parts for your application. Some kits come supplied with fitting brackets; however, others simply use ties which poke through the radiator's cooling fins to pull the fan tight to the core.

The first decision that must be made is twofold: size and location. Depending on the depth of the fan, it may be possible to mount it on the front of the radiator, behind the grille. This is a neat solution and allows plenty of clearance in the engine bay for other components. The author's supercharged Morris Minor has the fan mounted in this manner to allow clearance for the supercharger drive belt, for example. The disadvantage here is that this

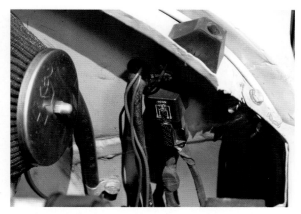

…and is supplied with its own relay and wiring sub-loom.

prevents the possibility of the radiator being lifted directly up and out, without removing the front panel, as there is insufficient clearance between the front of the fan and the front of the engine for the combined depth of the radiator core and fan to clear.

With the fan fitted, attention must turn to a means of switching it. A dash-mounted toggle switch is a useful override; however, as a primary solution, this is a risky strategy. If an increase in water temperature is missed by the driver, and the fan is not turned on, the engine may overheat.

A thermostatically controlled switch, then, is a logical solution. Basic units rely on a probe inserted under a jubilee clip and into a hose. This is not the most elegant solution and can often leak. A much more refined option is a fan controller, which mounts inline with the bottom hose. Kits such as those from Revotec come complete with a relay and wiring sub-loom, but if you are building your set-up from parts, it is important to note that the fan is a high-draw item and that a relay is essential for its safe operation. The fan should be wired into the permanent live circuit, with a fuse close to the battery, so that it continues to run and cool the car even once the ignition has been turned off. It is also important to remember when wiring the fan that if it is on the front of the radiator, its wires should be connected so that it pushes air towards the back of the car, through the radiator fins, whereas if it is fitted on the engine side of the radiator, it should be wired so that it sucks air through the radiator core. If a temperature gauge is fitted (*see* Chapter 14), the thermostatic fan control switch should be adjusted to kick-in just as the temperature needle creeps above 'Normal'.

LIGHTING UPGRADES

When the Morris Minor was built, its dim headlights were comparable with nearly every other vehicle on the road. Indeed, the Lucas 7-inch light unit was fitted to everything from the Morris Minor to Aston Martin DB4, Routemaster Bus to Mini and a great deal else in between. As lighting technology improved, sealed beam versions of these popular headlights became available, which offered more light output but with the drawback that the entire lamp needed replacing when the filament failed.

H4 halogen upgrades have become a cheap and common fitment to replace the original Lucas units, which use a standard H4 Halogen bulb to produce a much improved light and beam pattern. The greater draw of more powerful halogen bulbs does, however, increase load on the switch and, so, it is a good idea to introduce a relay to your headlight wiring to remove the loading of the switch and allow a higher-load light to be run safely.

Most recently, however, it has become possible to further improve the lighting of the Minor by fitting LED versions of the H4 bulb to the H4 light unit. The benefits of LEDs are twofold: improved performance and reduced electrical load (and thus no need for a relay as would be desirable for a conventional halogen bulb with equivalent light output). Although cheap upgrades are available, it is the experience of the author that they will not produce a satisfactory beam pattern and therefore would fail an MOT test as well as being dangerously dazzling to other motorists.

Lucas 7-inch headlights can be easily swapped for H4 halogen units, which in turn can now be fitted with LED bulbs. When choosing LED headlight bulbs, ensure that they have been designed to produce a proper beam pattern in an older light, or they will fail an MOT.

Clear sidelight/indicators for the later (post '63) front lamp units are a popular choice for modified cars, but note that an orange colour bulb must be fitted for the indicators. Spotlights are also a popular fitment.

'Halo' LED headlights which incorporate sidelights and indicators into the unit are a little 'Marmite' aesthetically, but the range of functions is impressive.

Sidelight bulbs are available in bright or warm white as a direct replacement for the filament bulb originals, and bright orange LED bulbs are available for the indicators.

Early Minors were not originally fitted with flashing indicators, instead relying on Trafficators, which are seldom seen these days. Additional indicators, therefore, are commonly found on regularly used Minors.

Here, an orange bulb has been used behind a clear lens, with the lamp unit fitted on a bracket below the bumper to provide flashing indicators without fitting a lamp unit to the rear wing as in the previous image.

Another clever upgrade from www.bettercarlighting.co.uk, the twin pole LED bulb here hides behind the original pre-'62 sidelight lens (with a double contact bulb holder). It lights warm white with sidelights, but is interrupted by a bright orange light when the indicators are switched on.

This ingenious set-up from www.bettercarlighting.co.uk incorporates a bright flashing orange indicator, bright red tail, and even brighter red brake lights into the early rear light unit for a completely concealed upgrade.

A high-level brake light is a sensible upgrade, given the towering height of modern SUVs.

Specialist classic car lighting companies such as www. bettercarlighting.co.uk, www.dynamoregulatorconversions.com or Stella Lux can offer LED H4 conversions which produce up to 30,000 lumen output while being designed to produce a proper beam pattern from within the Lucas 7-inch unit. These upgrades are also available in warm white as well as the blue white most commonly associated with LED lighting, putting them more in-keeping with the aesthetic of the Morris Minor.

Sidelights, brake lights and indicators, too, may be upgraded to LED bulbs, which are available in bright white, warm white, orange and red depending on the application from a great number of suppliers at a variety of price points and quality.

Hazard warning light kits are available from a number of suppliers and should be high on the priority list for any Minor owner.

There are also some clever conversions on the market to enable discreet indicators to be fitted to earlier Minors for which flashing indicators front and rear were not standard fitment. For example, www.bettercarlighting.co.uk offer dual-pole sidelight bulbs for the front which offer warm white sidelights until the indicator circuit is activated, at which point an interrupter circuit in the bulb cancels the sidelight and replaces it with a bright orange light. At the rear, conversions that use LED lightboards to incorporate bright orange flashing indicators alongside LED brake and tail lights are a neat and effective option.

Similarly, trafficator bulbs may be upgraded to flashing orange 'Flashicator' bulbs, available from www.dynamoregulatorconversions.com, which incorporate a flashing circuit in the bulb itself alongside bright orange LEDs.

Interior lighting may also be upgraded by means of an LED festoon bulb which, as well as offering far greater light output than the original, will run much cooler, preventing further degradation of the fragile plastic from which the Minor's interior light lens is manufactured.

As an aside, the sidelight circuit was never protected by a fuse prior to 1962 and fitting one is a sensible upgrade to avoid fried wiring caused by a short-circuit, a common occurrence with aged rear lights and dodgy seals. The author has first-hand experience of this, with a short-circuit in the number plate light of his recently restored Minor convertible causing a large section of his wiring loom from the rear of the car to front bulkhead to melt and require replacement. The simplest solution here is to install an inline fuse between the switch and sidelight circuit, which protects the long run of cable and most common points of failure – the rear lights – against a short circuit. Similarly, the headlights are not fused on any Minor. Fuses and relays can be introduced here, but it is recommended that each side is fused individually to avoid complete loss of lighting at night if the fuse were to blow.

ELECTRIC WASHERS

The standard mechanical pump in the Minor's dash is poor at best when it comes to reliably delivering a useful quantity of screenwash to the front glass. Happily, upgrading to a 12-volt electric washer pump with a momentary switch is the work of just a couple of hours, can cost as little as a few pounds, and is a straightforward enough conversion to be within the reach of even the least experienced mechanic.

This discreetly-fitted electric washer pump proves that modifications need not detract from a smart engine bay.

Reservoirs with built-in pumps are a simple solution, or alternatively if you want to keep your installation discreet, a small electrically-operated pump may be fitted inline from the original reservoir.

Note that not all Minors were fitted with washers from the factory. However, in order to be legal, all must be fitted with washers for use on the roads of today (apart from early post office vans with opening windscreens). The same, incidentally, goes for rear reflectors.

Starting at the reservoir, either a replacement reservoir with an integrated pump should be installed or an in-line pump should be added in the engine bay. If the latter option is used, a non-return foot valve must be added at the bottom of the system, pushed into the hose inside the reservoir. The hose should be cut and motor plumbed inline, noting 'in' and 'out' markings on the motor.

We are assuming here, of course, that there is sufficient slack in the existing run of tubing to simply splice the new motor into the existing system. If this is not the case with your Minor, you will need either to reposition your original reservoir, fit a reservoir with an integral motor, or replace the hose either in part or in its entirety.

Behind the dashboard, the original manual pump should be removed and the hoses that formerly entered and exited it should be connected together using a fuse box. The wire from the switch should be fed through a grommet in the bulkhead and neatly run to the washer motor. The other terminal on the washer motor should be connected to the car's body 'earth'.

With the motor wired and plumbed, it may be necessary to bleed the system to remove any air locked between the motor and the reservoir. If air locks continue to develop in the system, it may be necessary to add a second non-return valve to the system, just above the motor.

INERTIA SWITCH – FUEL PUMP

In the event of an accident in your Minor in which the fuel line is severed, fuel may be pumped over the hot exhaust until the ignition is switched off or the battery is disconnected by emergency services. Fitting an inertia switch to the fuel pump supply, as is common practice on all modern vehicles, mitigates this risk. The inertia switch must be accessible to be re-set in the event that it triggers in the event of heavy braking or after an accident once any immediate danger has been averted. As such, the most convenient point for it to be mounted is adjacent to the pump on the Minor's bulkhead. One wire to the switch should be connected to the pump's power feed, the other to the terminal to which this power lead would ordinarily be fitted. Adding this safety device should take less than an hour, and cost less than fifteen pounds for the switch and any wiring required.

Note that some switches are designed to be fitted to a multi-plug and therefore a male plug fitting must be sourced. Plugs with short leads pre-wired are readily available online or, alternatively, a switch may be sourced with these included. Although it is a modification which, with any luck, will never be required, it offers an additional level of protection against fire in the event of an accident and, therefore, is a sensible safety upgrade.

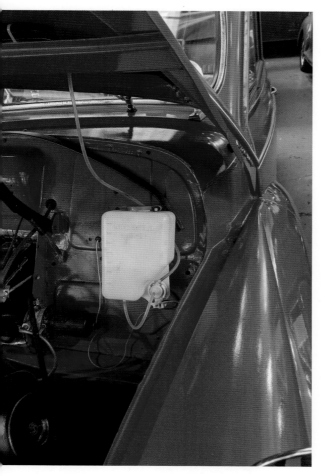

Washer-fluid reservoirs with inbuilt pumps make installation straightforward. They are often supplied as kits including wiring sub-looms and momentary contact switches.

straight pipe connector. A momentary contact switch should then be fitted in its place. One wire to the switch should be fed from the ignition-fused side of the Minor's

13

Are You Sitting Comfortably?

Driver and passenger comfort should be high on the priority list when thinking about what modifications you might like to make to your Morris Minor. Inside, after all, is where you will spend most of your time.

There is much to like about the Minor's charmingly basic interior comforts, but for those of us who have grown to expect a little more in terms of safety, comfort and adjustability, a standard Minor can leave much to be desired. There are simple solutions at a variety of price points to bring your Minor kicking and screaming into at least the latter part of the 20th century.

SEATS

Although the Minor's original seats are both aesthetically pleasing and moderately comfortable – at least when in good condition – they offer very little in terms of adjustability. The driver's seat has some position adjustment by means of a spring-loaded lever and both front seats can be moved back and forth on a semi-permanent basis by means of a number of captive nut options in the floor; however, there is no headrest fitted, meaning severe whiplash injuries or worse could be sustained in the event of a crash. To this end, many owners have opted to fit aftermarket seats, or seats removed from more modern cars, especially if high annual mileage is to be undertaken and adjustability on runners is desired for driver comfort and rear-seat leg room. A comfortable seat can mean the difference between being able to use a Morris Minor and the car sitting in the garage for many owners, and so a little investment here can be greatly beneficial to the overall enjoyment of the car. Costs of upgrades vary and so do the quality of installations. It should be noted that any upgraded front seat will be bulkier than the original seats and so rear leg room will be impeded, so consider how often you carry rear-seat passengers. Traveller owners should also take into account that the folding rear bench seat requires a significant amount of space to roll forward and so this must be considered when deciding on the position and depth of the front seats to be fitted.

There is no shortage of options when it comes to upgrading your Minor's seating, with the challenge being striking a balance between comfort, cost, simplicity and aesthetic.

The most common seat upgrade, and one which was developed specifically for the Morris Minor many years ago, is the offering from Newton Commercial (www.newtoncomm.co.uk). The company's 'Suffolk' seats are beautifully crafted in the UK, available in a range of colours to match your Minor's existing interior, feature headrests and moulded side bolsters for additional lumbar support. They are supplied on a sub-frame which bolts to the Minor's original seat mounts and requires just a pair of holes drilling at the rear of each seat to bolt through, making them likely the simplest seat upgrade available and well within the capabilities of most owners. Rear seat

…and can be supplied with rear seats to match, in a range of colour schemes.

Newton Commercial's 'Suffolk' seats offer bolt-in simplicity, comfort and pleasing aesthetic…

covers are available to match the Suffolk design and there is even an option for the front seats to be upgraded to become heated if desired. These seats are undoubtedly a great upgrade for any Morris Minor; however, they do represent a significant investment at almost seven hundred pounds each including VAT for vinyl versions at the time of writing, with leather-faced and heated options available at an additional cost.

For those seeking a cheaper alternative, many owners choose to re-purpose seats from more modern cars, with seats from the Ford KA having become a common choice in recent years thanks to their relative compactness, comfort and availability as the little Ford disappears from Britain's roads. Three of the KA's four original mounting feet can even be re-purposed for use in the Minor. All the feet are riveted to the runners, so

these must first be drilled out and removed, then the feet rearranged so that the two matching offset feet, originally on the inside edge of the KA seat, may be turned 180 degrees and bolted to the front of the runners facing inwards to match with the original holes in the Minor's floor pan. At the rear, the large foot can be cut in half vertically before being reinstalled one half on the back of each runner, with a hole for each being the only modification required to the Minor's bodywork. In one of his own Minors, the author has gone one step further and utilised a set of heated black leather Ford Street KA-derived seats which incorporate a conveniently placed and discreet switch for their operation and merely require a 12-volt fused and relayed input and an earth wire connecting to one of the seat mounting bolts. These seats make the car a pleasure to drive in winter months and allow the full (yet feeble) power of the heater to be directed at the windscreen.

Bolt-in subframes are supplied with Newton Commercial seats to make installation simple.

Ford KA seats have proved a popular budget conversion in recent years. Here, KA rear seats have been installed to complement the fronts.

Ford's Street KA featured heated seats, making them a desirable donor.

MGF seats can be purchased cheaply enough and, thanks to the donor car's retro styling, don't look out of place in the Minor.

MGF Seats are another option, and are not dissimilar in design and comfort to the Newton Commercial Suffolk seats. A sub-frame will require making for these to fit, as

BB Classics' Vintage Bucket Seats offer plenty of side-to-side support and are popular with those seeking a hot rod look.

with many other modern seat options, but this should not be beyond the skills of most competent home mechanics. The MGF was designed with a nod to the firm's sports cars of old, so the overall look of the seats fits well with the Minor's aesthetic and, with access to the mid-mounted engine in the F part of the original design brief, the seats incorporate a forward tilting mechanism, too, making rear seat access simple.

Aftermarket seats designed for kit cars such as the vintage-style bucket seats from BB Classics (www. bbclassics.co.uk) are popular with those going for the 'hot rod' look, and offer a decent level of side-to-side location thanks to their figure-hugging design. However, they are narrow and may not be comfortable for all body shapes. But if you fit them, these are a very comfortable and sporting option, well in keeping with the Minor's aesthetic and even available with heating elements for those cold winter months. Clubsport and GT seats are also available from the same supplier, with head rests for a modicum of crash safety.

SEAT BELTS

Seat belt mounting points were incorporated into the Minor's bodyshell from August 1961 for the 1962 model year, although static front seatbelts were not fitted, except as optional dealer-fitted extras, until they became a legal requirement in 1971.

Bodies modified to accept seat belts bear the following numbers: 2-door saloon, 362117 to 362200 and 362295 onwards; 4-door saloon, 204617 onwards; Convertible, 66338 to 66400 and 66467 onwards; Travellers, 90769 onwards.

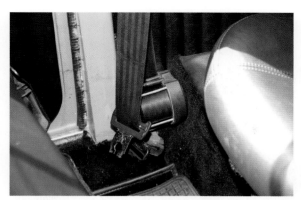

Both static and inertia reel seat belts can be fitted to the Minor, with kits available at a modest cost.

In the rear of a saloon, the back parcel shelf is often used as a belt mounting point.

Fitting seat belts to a car with this provision, then, is a relatively straightforward task, and upgrading from static to inertia reel type belts is just as easy, and an upgrade which adds both convenience and a modicum of safety to your Minor.

Earlier Minors can, of course, be fitted with front seat belts too, by replicating the mounting points later incorporated by the factory into the car's shell. This is a complex and safety critical job, however, so should be tackled by a qualified and competent person.

There was never any factory provision for rear seatbelts, but many owners have fitted them with varying degrees of neatness. The most common installation point for an inertia reel-type rear seat belt is on the rear parcel shelf of saloon models, with buckles fastened to the floor below the rear seat base, stalks protruding between the seat base and back. In Traveller models, rear belt reels are often mounted on the inner wheel arches.

Any seat belt installation, of course, relies on the vehicle structure being in sound condition and the belts themselves having been fitted such that they will operate as intended in the case of an accident. It should also be noted that the Minor's bodyshell, having been designed in the 1940s, was not designed with the same levels of passenger safety in mind as modern vehicles and so, although belts will help in the case of an accident, they do not bring the Morris Minor inline with modern safety standards.

In a traveller, rear belts are most commonly mounted to the rear wheel arch. It is recommended that any seat belt conversion is carried out by a qualified engineer.

14

Mod Cons

GAUGES

Fitting aftermarket gauges to your Morris Minor is a great way to keep an eye on what is happening under the bonnet. Oil pressure and water temperature are a must when it comes to ensuring your engine is, and remains, in fine fettle, while an ammeter can be useful for ensuring that power demand does not outstrip supply from the charging system. A voltmeter (perhaps even in the form of a digital gauge built into an accessory docket) can give an early indication of a failing battery or charging system, while a rev counter, sometimes referred to as a tachometer, can be helpful if your ears are not mechanically empathetic. Meanwhile, vacuum economy gauges are novel but not necessary if a little mechanical sympathy is observed.

Positioning of gauges in a Minor can be tricky – go to any rally and you will find examples of various positions and executions, each with their own advantages and disadvantages. There is no 'perfect location'. Discreet fitment is often desirable, but gauges should also be easily seen by the driver. Commonly the glovebox behind the steering wheel is utilised for gauges, but this has the disadvantage of lost storage as well as inhibiting access to the speedometer head securing screws.

Accessory brackets are available for under-dash mounting, which is a neat and simple solution. However, this

For a more subtle look, gauges may be mounted beneath the dashboards.

1098 and 1275 'heads both feature water temperature sensor drillings. These are not present on standard 948 cylinder heads.

Gauges should be mounted so that they are easily visible from the driver's seat.

does mean that the driver must glance further away from the road to check the gauges.

Oil pressure gauges may either be controlled via an electronic sender or a pressure-fed line direct to the rear of the gauge. In both instances, a connection must be made to the oil pressure sender drilling, originally fitted with just the oil pressure light switch, to the rear of the block just above the distributor. A screw-in direct T-piece or remote T-piece (recommended, as direct Ts can cause clearance issues with the distributor if timing adjustments

A remote T-piece allows both oil pressure gauge and light senders to be fitted without fouling on the distributor.

Late Mini heaters feature two-speed fans – perfect for providing a little more warmth in your Minor's cabin.

are required) may be used to retain the original low oil pressure warning light (in the speedometer head) alongside a gauge. Note that remote T-pieces may need to be electrically earthed if there is no conductive connection to the block to enable the oil pressure switch and/or an electronic sender to function.

Water temperature gauges, as well, may either be electrically controlled or via a direct connection. Older-style gauges use a capillary tube hard-plumbed to the rear of the gauge head, whereas more modern types use an electronic sender wired to the gauge. In the case of the latter, it is important that the gauge and sender are correctly matched and wired correctly (via an instrument voltage stabiliser if required, as fitted to the rear of the speedometer to regulate voltage to the fuel gauge on later Minors), to ensure that a correct reading is given.

HEATER UPGRADES

Early Minors used a round, re-circulating heater that was better than nothing, although not particularly effective at either clearing the windscreen or warming the cabin. 1098 models from late 1963 saw a great improvement in passenger comfort with the introduction of a square-fronted heater with a fresh air intake via trunking from just behind the front grille. However, even this is rather poor by modern standards. A similarly-designed heater was fitted to the classic Mini, which remained in production until 2000 and, as such, was required to evolve with the times.

Austin Rover's solution to this problem was to introduce a more efficient heater matrix of the same dimensions as the original, which can be retro-fitted to the Minor's heater, improving its effectiveness greatly. Similarly, the entire Mini heater unit may be fitted to allow

your Minor to benefit from the twin-speed fan introduced into the later Minis.

If your heater is particularly poor, it may benefit simply from a flush to remove years of corrosion and debris from the matrix. To do this, remove both heater hoses from the engine and drain out all traces of coolant, which can be hazardous to the environment. Connect one of the disconnected hoses to a garden hose, and point the other to the floor. Allow water to flow through the matrix until the water coming out the other end runs clear, then reverse the operation. Repeat the process until the matrix is completely clean. In the same way, the radiator and engine block can also be flushed to ensure efficient cooling of the engine. Similarly, it is worth installing an 88-degree Celsius thermostat for winter months, replacing this with an 82-degree item for summer driving.

RADIO/ICE

Fitting some form of in-car entertainment to your Minor has never yielded so much choice. Whether you are looking to fit a conventional head unit or a bluetooth transmitter, or even just an amplifier which your mobile phone plugs into, there is a world of options available to you. Most Minor owners stick to a conventional head unit, mounted either in a glovebox or below the dashboard; however, even here there remains a key choice: modern or retro.

Modern head units can look out of place in an older car, and so a number of suppliers have developed a range of retro-styled head units that incorporate modern internals, thus giving the user the best of both worlds.

Wiring is almost identical for each of the options available to you. A battery live, to preserve settings and play memory; an ignition live, to power the unit when the ignition key

Radio head units are often concealed within gloveboxes.

Bluetooth amplifiers provide a neat alternative to a traditional head unit.

Retro-design head units offer a compromise of aesthetic vs performance.

With both speaker and battery technology progressing apace, don't discount the idea of simply taking a Bluetooth speaker along for the ride.

is switched on; a good earth and, finally, speaker wiring. All modern ICE offerings will rely on the vehicle already being wired as negative earth (*see* Chapter 12).

The earth is easy, using a ring terminal with a screw into the bodywork of the car. Ignition and permanent battery live feeds should be taken from the fused side of the fusebox, high up on the left-hand side of the bulkhead when viewed from the front of the car. Identify which is which using a test light or multimeter with the fuses removed.

Speaker positioning can be tricky, but a variety of solutions have been successfully employed by owners seeking tunes on the go. Below the dashboard, access holes in the sheet metal pressing may be covered over with plywood into which speakers are fitted. Alternatively, or in addition, the kidney panel pressings behind the front kick plates in the footwells offer sufficient depth for a small set of speakers. Two-door rear trim panels are often cut to accommodate speakers, and speaker boxes are commonly fitted on the rear parcel shelf, too. Finally, some owners cut

the cross-member in front of the rear seat to fit 6 x 9 inch speakers, although questions have been raised about the effect of this on the vehicle's structure, while others have made plywood speaker boxes that fit below the standard Minor seats.

Of course, with the advent of powerful modern battery-powered bluetooth speakers, many owners are now choosing to use one of these instead of a hard-wired radio. Requiring no wiring, no cutting or fitting of speakers, these are a simple, cheap and effective solution to the in-car entertainment problem.

12-VOLT ACCESSORY SOCKETS

Keeping electronic devices such as mobile phones and satellite navigation systems charged has become essential in the modern age, and so a 12-volt accessory socket is a handy addition to your Minor, which can be discreetly wired and positioned either beneath the dash or inside a glovebox for maximum discretion.

As our reliance on technology has increased, so has the need to charge our devices. A 12-volt accessory socket has become almost essential.

Gone are the days when a cigarette lighter socket is the only option, and a variety of self-contained, pre-wired units are now available, some even incorporating USB charging ports, with moulded mounting plinths integral to their design.

It is recommended that accessory sockets be wired to the ignition live circuit, to prevent the battery being flattened if a charger is left plugged in overnight, and independently fused to prevent overloading the ignition live fuse, which powers the indicators, brake lights, wipers and indicators.

SOUND DEADENING

Tap the roof or door of your Minor and it will ring like a church bell. That same resonance will translate into unpleasant amplification of road and drivetrain noise on the move, making the driving experience very noisy. Modern cars are equipped with copious amounts of sound-deadening materials, which insulate the occupants from the outside world. Adding sound deadening to your Minor, then, will improve the overall feel of the car as well as driver and passenger comfort, making the Minor that much more appealing for regular use and longer journeys.

Before carrying out any sound-deadening work, consider whether your Minor is structurally sound, or whether it will require any welding work in the near future. If welding work is to be undertaken in the vicinity of sound-deadening materials, they must first be removed from the area, so it pays to ensure that this will not be required for many years to come. Scraping bituminous material from rusty steel panels is not a fun task, and removing even recently installed sticky sound deadening renders it fit only for the bin – a waste of time and money!

During a restoration is the most obvious time to go mad with the sound-deadening materials, as if the car is stripped to a bare shell, it is far more straightforward to apply, given that much of the stripdown required to access floors, bulkheads, door and roof panels has already been done as part of the restoration. Having said that, a Minor is not the most complex car to deconstruct and therefore applying sound-deadening materials can be an enjoyable end-of-season weekend task.

Bituminous sound-deadening pads, such as Dynamat, DodoMat, Silent Coat and others can be applied directly to steel panels and deaden sound by acting as a vibration damper that stops the panel 'ringing'.

Foam-based insulation atop this can insulate both heat and road noise transmission, too, and the closed-cell construction of most modern foam insulation means that water retention is not so much of an issue as with original-type underfelt, which can trap moisture against the car's floor panels and cause corrosion.

HEATED SCREENS

Heated screens are available for the front and rear of your Minor, and are a sensible upgrade if you plan on using your Minor in all weathers, with the necessity to scrape ice from the inside as well as the outside of the car's glass quite common in winter months. Note that these screens draw a significant amount of current, and so upgrading your Minor to an alternator before fitting one, or both, heated screens is essential to avoid discharging the battery faster than it is recharged. Note, too, that these are likely to be used when the car is running but not moving, therefore the alternator's ability to charge while the car is at idle is a substantial benefit over the dynamo.

Generic wiring kits are available, but making your own is not out of the reach of most home mechanics. Drawing around 13.5 amps, a minimum of 10-gauge wire (for 30-amp circuits) should be used throughout for safety, allowing the safe use of a 20-amp fuse. A toggle switch and some form of warning light (either on the dash, or integrated into the switch) will be required as well as a relay. Some more modern classics use a timer relay for this application, which not only reduces the load on the switch but also cuts power to the screen after a predetermined (or in some cases adjustable by means of a trimming resistor) time period, mitigating the risk of the heated screen being left on and draining the battery or burning out its filaments. If a timer relay is to be used, a momentary switch may be used in place of a toggle switch. The circuit should also be fused – consider choosing a relay with an inbuilt fuse to keep the wiring neat and tidy.

WIPER UPGRADES

If you plan on using your Morris Minor regularly, a major benefit is upgrading the windscreen wipers. The original single-speed wiper motor leaves much to be desired in a heavy rain storm, where the wipers cannot keep pace with the amount of water that requires clearing from the screen. Similarly, in light drizzle, flicking the switch on and off can be a frustrating necessity. To this end, let's look at how both intermittent and twin-speed wiper motor conversions can be incorporated into the Minor, either in isolation or as a neat and modern pairing.

Twin-speed Wipers

Twin-speed wiper conversions are straightforward and well worthwhile, with kits available to enable the use of Lucas twin-speed motors as used on other cars in the BMC and BL model range available from a number of specialists. Alternatively, a second-hand motor may be sourced from an autojumble or online and the kit built from component parts.

Before embarking on upgrading the wipers on your Minor, first it is important to consider the switching methods used in your particular car from standard and therefore the options available to you for upgrades. Prior to 1963, pull switches were used. Wipers used a simple 'off/on' switch whereas lights used 'off/on/on' switches which allowed the sidelights to be turned on independently from main headlights. The 'W' and 'L' markings on the bakelite knobs differentiate the switch functions for the driver; however, with a small screwdriver or pick, a sprung pin underneath the switch may be depressed so that the knob may be removed. As such, if a twin-position light switch is desired for use on the wiper circuit (for twin-speed wipers), a 'W' knob may be used in place of the original 'L' knob, allowing the original in-car aesthetic to be maintained while adding an extra function. Similarly on post-'63 cars, where toggle switches are used, wipers use 'on/off' and lights use 'off/on/on' switches. In this case, there is no marking on the switches and therefore using a twin-position light switch for the wipers is completely straightforward.

Also note that pre-October 1963 Minors used 'clap hand'-style wipers and require a different sweep angle to be produced by the wiper motor's driven gear, so this will need to be considered when choosing a suitable motor for your conversion.

A complete kit for conversion to dual-speed wipers (ESM Part number WPR201) costs around £150 at the time of writing, and contains everything required to convert a post October '63 Minor, including instructions, a wiring sub-loom, motor, bracket and switch.

Intermittent Wipers

Intermittent wipers have become ubiquitous on modern cars, and for good reason. A simple interrupter circuit is used to make and break the wiper circuit when intermittent speed is selected on the wiper switch. In the past, Minor owners have used simple electronics and adjustable timer relays to achieve intermittent wipers for their cars, but more recently a UK-based company, Retronics Ltd (www.retronicsonline.co.uk) have developed a kit specifically for the purpose of fitting intermittent wipers to classic cars. The kit offers sweep intervals of 2, 3, 4, 8 and 12 seconds, adjustable by means of a rotary switch which

Twin-speed wipers make all the difference in heavy rain.

Off-the-shelf conversion kits are available for post-'63 cars.

mounts neatly on the dashboard. The author suggests that the most convenient and neatest mounting location on a post-'62 Minor would be directly next to the wiper switch in the hole originally used for the windscreen washer pump which, if upgraded to electric, could have its momentary switch relocated either vertically beneath the speedometer or horizontally on a separate bracket beneath the dash. Comprehensive fitting instructions and wiring diagrams are included with the Retronics kit, making fitting a reasonably straightforward process for most DIYers.

Going Further

If you were feeling really ambitious, it would not be the most difficult task in the world to wire a windscreen rain sensor into the wiper circuit. In this case, a rain sensor from a donor car must be sourced and mounted inconspicuously on the screen (e.g. behind the rear-view mirror). The sensor is simply a switch that must be wired via a relay to the wiper circuit. An additional position on the switch must be used to facilitate this, in which case a five-position rotary switch will be the neatest solution if off, rain-sensing, intermittent, slow and fast speeds are to be incorporated into the circuit. Alternatively, separate switches for rain sensing and intermittent could be added beneath the dashboard or even conversion to stalk-based

Intermittent wiper kits are also available, and come complete with detailed wiring instructions.

controls may be considered to give the Minor a more modern feel and allow more controls to be incorporated without cluttering up the dash. Identifying requirements and controls from a car in the MG Rover group would be a good place to start.

15

Towing With Your Minor

Many Morris Minor owners opt to fit tow bars, often for towing camping trailers, trailer tents, small caravans or even as a mounting point for bike racks. A wide variety of bars are available to buy, and fitting should be well within the capabilities of a DIY mechanic.

Crucially, the areas surrounding the tow bar's mounting points should be inspected carefully for signs of corrosion, and the tow bar's fitting instructions followed to the letter.

The maximum specified towing capacity for a Minor is 1,344lb, or 609.5kg. Consider upgrading your Minor's

A tow bar is a handy addition, whether for towing or as a mounting point for a bike rack.

A trailer tent is a popular choice for towing behind a Minor.

Small caravans are harder to tow, although they may be within the Minor's weight limit, due to wind resistance.

brakes to be able to arrest this additional momentum and also note that trailers are available with their own brakes triggered by the compression of the hitch mechanism, which makes slowing far safer.

Wiring to the rear lights should be reasonably straightforward, with feeds taken from the right hand side of the boot space where the main wiring loom connects to the rear lights. Wiring diagrams are provided with all towing electrics, or easily found on the web. Note that an audible buzzer should be fitted in line between the indicator feeds and towing socket to alert the driver that the lights are working correctly. These are cheaply and easily available online.

If you intend on towing a trailer with a reasonably heavy nose weight regularly, you may want to consider upgrading to stiffer rear springs and firmer bushes (*see* Chapter 11), to handle this additional weight more effectively. Similarly, the additional weight will put strain on your Minor's engine and, with the legal top speed for towing a trailer being 50mph (80km/h) on single and 60mph (97km/h) on dual carriageways, a lower ratio final drive, such as a 4.55:1 unit from a pre-'62 Minor may be considered if you plan on towing for much of the time. Unless the engine has been heavily upgraded, a Minor with a 3.9:1 final drive will struggle to tow a reasonably heavy trailer up any incline.

16

Body Modifications

GRP BODY PANELS

Rust is the enemy with any classic car, no less so with the Minor. Wings front and rear, boot lid, front valance and both bumper valances are common rot spots, which can be eliminated easily without changing the overall look of the car by using fibreglass panels. These are available in a range of price points and qualities.

The fibreglass panels sold by JLH Morris Minors are widely regarded as being the best fitting of all those available. These feature aesthetically modified panels including front wings which incorporate flared arches; widened rear wings; smoothed boot lids without a number plate recess; a full flip front available within the range alongside replacement fibreglass front wings for both high and low headlight cars; rear wings for saloons and Travellers; bumper valances; and both Minor 1000- and Series II-style front panels which, once painted, would be hard to tell apart from a steel item.

WEATHER STRIPS

The standard felt seals that touch either side of the Morris Minor's sliding door glass are great at preventing pebbles from entering the door skin, but less good at keeping water

…touch-glass type seals do not.

out. The theory is that a plastic weather sheet stuck to the metalwork of the door prevents the door card warping and holes in the bottom of the door allow any water that has made its way in, to find its way out. In reality, weather sheets have invariably either become detached or torn over the years, meaning that door cards warp, and drain holes block up, ensuring that the door corrodes inexorably.

Touch glass window weather strips, as fitted to all modern cars, are the answer here. They work on the principle that prevention is better than cure and keep all but the worst rain out. Fitting is fiddly, but well within the skill set of most enthusiast owners, and the difference in terms of interior and exterior longevity is well worth the effort. Having said that, they do not replace the need to keep drain holes in the bottom of the doors clear, weather sheets firmly stuck and cavity wax topped up regularly.

CHOP-TOP CONVERTIBLES

Not something to be covered in great detail here, but something to be aware of, is the relative simplicity of converting a two-door Minor saloon to a convertible. Much has been covered elsewhere and, if you are interested in converting your two-door Morris Minor into a convertible, kits are available to do just that with detailed instructions available alongside.

Original-type felt weather strips allow water into the inside of the door…

Genuine convertibles display 'T' in their chassis number, in place of '2S' for a two-door saloon. However, plates can be easily changed.

Check strengthening gussets for factory spot welds. B-pillar is hardest to replicate.

It is worth noting that if you are looking to purchase a Minor convertible, there are some superbly converted saloons out there, and in terms of day-to-day use and enjoyment, there is little to no difference between a genuine convertible and a chopped saloon. The values of original drop-tops, however, are significantly higher than their converted counterparts and so care must be taken when buying to avoid paying over the odds for a replica.

Original convertibles are identifiable first by a 'T' in their chassis number, found on an aluminium plate screwed to the bulkhead, which denotes 'Tourer' (early cars had removable side-screens and were, therefore, classed as tourers rather than convertibles). An 'MA2...' chassis number denotes that the car was originally a two-door saloon. These plates are easily removed, however, and there are numerous cases of the identities of rotten genuine convertibles being assigned to converted cars by unscrupulous people. Another key indicator is that the strengthening fillets (beneath the dash and at the base of the B posts) were spot-welded in place on original convertibles, but are often either seam- or plug-welded on conversions. Those which are likely to be the biggest giveaway are the rearmost B-pillar plate welds, where it is impossible to fit a domestic spot welder to replicate the factory welds at home. The final tell-tale is that the top of the windscreen frame on a genuine convertible is flat, whereas shop tops are often rounded, as per the profile of the original roof. As with ID plates, however, many rotten genuine convertibles have given up their screen tops to conceal the identity of a chopped saloon.

17

Other Accessories

It is rare to find two Morris Minors that are completely alike. Owners have been modifying and customising their cars for years, with a great many more customisation options available that we have not had space to discuss here, but which will become evident if you walk around any rally field.

Aesthetic modifications such as custom paint, external sun visors, front spoilers and others are among the more radical bolt-on personal touches, while spot lamps, mirrors and locking fuel filler caps combine aesthetic with practical applications. Depending on the sort of use your Minor gets, you may also consider the addition of a larger capacity petrol tank, too.

The most important thing to remember is that it is *your* car. Your tastes will likely not be the same as everyone else's, but it is your enjoyment and love of the car that counts. Look around for inspiration, but do not be afraid to go your own way. And don't forget: such is the bolt-on nature of most aftermarket accessories, you can always revert back to standard if you change your mind.

The range of aftermarket accessories available for the Minor is impressive. These mudflaps help keep road dirt from the end-grain of this Traveller's rear pillar.

Locking fuel filler caps are a sensible upgrade, particularly if you use your Minor daily.

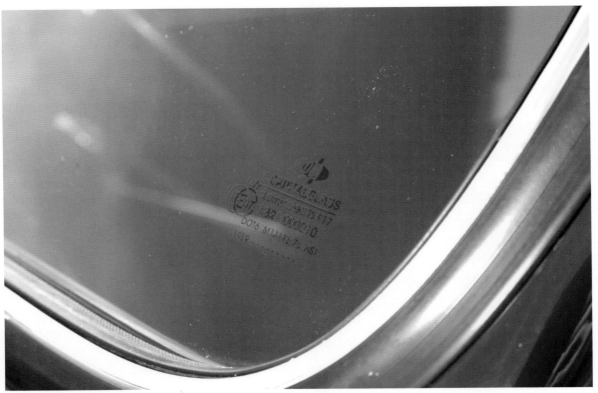

Laminated front screens offer much improved safety over toughened originals. A stone strike to a laminated screen will cause it to crack, whereas a toughened screen will shatter. Heated front and rear screens are also available.

Telescopic boot stay kits make loading and unloading far easier – particularly on a pre-'63 Minor with its manual prop.

A wide range of steering wheels has been fitted to Minors over the years. A smaller wheel will give faster steering response for the same input and a sportier feel, but will also make the steering heavier at low speed and limit control over bumps and shakes. This 14-inch Moto Lita combines stunning aesthetics with pleasant feel and great controllability.

While saloons and travellers offer great visibility, this is not shared with LCVs. Here, a reversing camera has been fitted below the number plate of the van featured elsewhere in this publication, which feeds a display concealed in the rear-view mirror.

Whether for aesthetic or practical purposes, a boot rack is a popular fitment to saloons and convertibles. Perfect for a picnic basket or additional luggage space for holidays, boot racks are held to the boot by tensioned hooks, so no drilling of the boot lid is required.

Case Studies

Each of these Minors has been modified to suit its owners wants and needs, and feature a variety of the everyday modifications described in this book.

Now we have explored the principles behind modifying the Morris Minor, let's take a look at how a few owners have employed the preceding theories in practice…

1960 MORRIS MINOR 998cc CONVERTIBLE

Technical Specifications

Engine: 948cc A-series over-bored to accept 998cc Mini pistons
Camshaft: MG Metro Turbo
Carburettor: HIF38
Exhaust: 1.5 inch 'big bore'
Manifold: Morris Marina cast combined inlet/exhaust
Gearbox: 1098 'ribbed case' Morris Minor gearbox
Ancillaries: Alternator conversion, electronic ignition, spin-on oil filter
Differential: 4.55:1
Brakes: Marina discs (front) Non-servo
Suspension upgrades: Polybush comfort bushes throughout, Morris Marina torsion bars, ride height lowered by

two inches at front, 1.5 inches at the rear.
Wheels and tyres: 4.5-inch reproduction Morris Minor van wheels; 145 HR 14 Pirelli Cinturato CA67

Impressions

The author's own car, this little convertible is a real delight to drive. The fully balanced 998cc engine (yes, you read that right, it is a 948 inline engine over-bored to take 998 Mini pistons) revs beautifully and is paired to a stronger ribbed case 1098-derived gearbox and the original 4.55:1 differential, resulting in a delightfully charming combination. Fulfilling a build brief to retain as much of the 1960 car's early Minor 1000 features and character as possible, the interior is correct for the year and neatly concealed gauges and bluetooth amplifier within the driver's side glovebox, behind a door for this model year, ensure a wonderfully authentic sensory experience from behind the wheel.

This is not a fast car, but it is certainly quicker than a standard 948cc Minor and far more usable for its improved braking, acceleration and handling characteristics. The original seven-inch front drum brakes have been replaced

The author's own 998cc Minor convertible is a delight to drive on country roads.

Original rear lights conceal LED stop/tail and indicator boards, keeping the rear of the car clean and uncluttered.

998cc A-series zips along keenly.

Is there a better place to be on a summer's day? Note the slightly lowered ride height front and rear.

by a Morris Marina-based disc brake set-up which pulls the car up beautifully and the Marina-derived torsion bars offer a decent spring rate despite the lowered ride height. At the rear, the stiffer torsion bars are balanced with seven-leaf springs from a Traveller with 1.5-inch lowering blocks between the spring and axle. Compliant comfort-grade suspension bushes from Polybush combined with a thorough sound-deadening campaign (Dynamat Xtreme was applied while the car was a bare shell and is complemented by Dynaliner closed cell foam underlay beneath the carpets) mean that this is a Minor in which voices need not be raised even at its top comfortable cruising speed of 62mph.

It really is a charming delight on country roads if a little under-geared for motorway cruising, due to the 4.55:1 differential. This has not stopped the author enjoying its delights on multiple trips as far afield as northern Spain and mid-west France.

1970 MORRIS MINOR 1098cc TRAVELLER

Technical Specifications

Engine: 1098cc A-series with 12G940 cylinder head
Camshaft: Kent 266
Carburettor: HIF44
Exhaust: 1.5 inch 'big bore'
Manifold: 1.5-inch cast aluminium Inlet, LCB tubular exhaust manifold
Gearbox: Type-9 Ford five-speed
Ancillaries: Alternator conversion; electronic ignition; electric cooling fan
Suspension: Lowered ride height front and rear (lowering blocks at rear, 1x spline at front), anti roll bar, polyurethane bushes throughout
Differential: 4.22:1
Brakes: Ford vented discs (front); no servo
Wheels and tyres: Banded steel wheels (5.5 inches); Continental Eco Contact 165/70R14

Impressions

A stunning example of the joys of a lightly modified 1098 engine, this Traveller gathers pace briskly enough with a lovely rasp from the stainless steel 1.5-inch exhaust. Some may consider the HIF44 fitted a little too large for the 1098, but the proof of the pudding is in the eating here and it runs superbly. Once up to speed, the Type 9 five-speed gearbox makes cruising relaxed while the red leather MGF seats and wooden steering wheel combine with plenty of sound-deadening materials used throughout to give a sense of real comfort and class. Vented disc brakes pull the car up sharply even without a servo to assist, and a slightly lower than standard ride height and wide wheels and tyres inspire confidence on the bends.

Owner Ian Kimpton explains:

> *'I wanted a Traveller that I could use and enjoy. I wasn't worried about originality and, having previously owned a standard 948cc-powered four-door Minor, was keen to have something with a lit-*

Ian Kimpton's 1970 Traveller has been modified with comfortable cruising in mind.

Mud flaps and reversing lights are just two of the modern twists up this Traveller's sleeve.

Spot lamps offer both aesthetic and practical improvements.

Speedy! By the time of our photoshoot, this Traveller had a rather highly-strung 1380 lump hiding beneath the bonnet.

Smartly appointed engine bay includes HIF44 carburettor and LCB tubular exhaust manifold.

tle more poke. The five-speed gearbox, MGF seats and sound deadening make this car a real joy to drive on a long journey.'

Note: Eagle-eyed readers will spot the lack of tappet chest covers and 12G940 cylinder head under the bonnet of this car elsewhere in this book. Between the author's road test and the time of our main photoshoot, the 1098cc engine had been removed and fitted to another Traveller of a remarkably similar specification, to be replaced by a rather highly-strung MG Midget-based 1380cc A-series

built by the author. Driving impressions are based on the 1098 engine.

1958 MORRIS MINOR *1275* VAN

Technical Specifications

Engine: 1275 MG Midget A-series
Camshaft: MG Metro (non-turbo)
Carburettor: HIF44
Exhaust: 1.5-inch 'big bore', side exit
Manifold: 1.75-inch cast aluminium inlet, LCB tubular exhaust manifold
Gearbox: Spridget ribbed case
Ancillaries: Alternator conversion, electronic ignition, electric cooling fan
Differential: 3.9:1
Suspension: Front lowered by 1.5 inches, eight-leaf springs on rear with lowering blocks
Brakes: Riley One-Point-Five 9-inch drums
Wheels and tyres: Banded steel wheels (5.5 inches); Toyo NanoEnergy 3 165/70/R14

Impressions

A proper 'old school' build, completed in 2021, this van is a real head-turner. Keeping aesthetic modifications in line with those of its era, owner Tom Morris has created something very special indeed. Fitted with pretty much the complete running gear from a 1275 MG Midget – engine,

Tom Morris's 1958 van is a triumph of aesthetic simplicity.

Sympathetic modifications make this van a real head-turner.

Flashing indicators are concealed in the rear reflectors.

5.5J banded steel wheels with smooth LCV hubcaps really look the part.

gearbox and differential – the HIF44 carburettor and full-flow tubular exhaust system allow the engine to breathe beautifully, allowing the van to pull with plenty of power right through the rev range. Banded steel wheels painted in the original birch grey with matching grille set the visual look and exemplify the benefits of uncluttered simplicity.

Being an early van, with small rear windows, rear visibility from standard is somewhat limited. Tom has fitted a reversing camera below the number plate (and concealed, detachable tow bar), as well as a parabolic lens to the nearside rear window, which is incredibly effective at improving rear visibility.

Inside, original seats and steering wheel complete the period-modified look, while oil pressure and water temperature gauges, as well as a rev counter and 12-volt accessory socket are discreetly mounted to allow modern benefits without upsetting the desired aesthetic. A very nicely built van indeed.

1970 MORRIS MINOR *SUPERCHARGED 1275* SALOON

Technical Specifications

Engine: 1275cc A-series over-bored for +0.040in Omega forged pistons with an 18cc dish
Camshaft: Piper METSC1
Carburettor: HIF44
Exhaust: 2 inch straight through (self-build)

Intake: Eaton M45 Supercharger
Gearbox: Type 9 Ford five-speed
Ancillaries: Alternator conversion, electronic ignition, spin-on oil filter
Differential: 4.22:1
Brakes: MGB calipers and pads, Marina discs; no servo
Suspension upgrades: Front: Morris Marina torsion bars; ARB; Rear: Seven-leaf Traveller springs; Telescopic dampers; anti-tramp bars. Performance grade Polybush suspension bushes throughout
Wheels and tyres: 4.5-inch reproduction Morris Minor van wheels; 165R14 84H Vredstein Sprint Classic

The author's supercharged Minor saloon is a wolf in sheep's clothing.

'Supercharged' badging hints at the monster within!

Reproduction van wheels with plain hubcaps suit the subtly modified look.

Eaton M45 supercharger gives this Moggie an impressive turn of speed.

Impressions

Another of the author's own collection, his first car in fact, the engine in this Minor has been built with reliable power in mind. The Eaton M45 supercharger, itself sourced from another product of the Cowley birthplace of the Minor, a BMW MINI Cooper S, feeds compressed air/fuel mixture into the 1275 Midget-based engine, such that both power and torque are quite staggering. Perhaps the ultimate development of the A-series, the driving experience is scintillating, with home-made anti-tramp bars combining with competition half-shafts to reliably and smoothly deliver power to the road. Stiffer and lower than standard suspension means that this beast handles well too, albeit without such a smooth ride as would have been experienced out of the factory. A Ford Sierra-derived type 9 five-speed gearbox feeding a 4.22:1 final drive enables relaxed high-speed cruising without compromising acceleration. A real wolf in sheep's clothing.

1961 MORRIS MINOR *1275* CONVERTIBLE

Technical Specifications

Engine: 1275 Ital A+
Camshaft: Swiftune SW5
Carburettor: HIF44
Exhaust: Maniflow 1.5 inch 'big bore'
Manifold: 1.75-inch cast aluminium inlet, LCB tubular exhaust manifold

Gearbox: Type-9 Ford Five-speed
Ancillaries: Alternator conversion; electronic ignition; electric cooling fan
Suspension: Front lowered by 1.5 inches with anti-roll bar, seven-leaf springs and lowering blocks at the rear. Telescopic dampers all round
Differential: 4.22:1
Brakes: Ford vented discs (front) with remote servo
Wheels and tyres: 15-inch 5½ in J Minilite style, 175/55/R15 Yokohama A.drive

Impressions

Emily Cook brought this superbly-modified Convertible along to our photoshoot. Fitted with an Ital-derived 1275 A+ mated to a type-9 five-speed gearbox with a 4.22:1 final drive, it really shifts and is happy cruising at the top end of the national speed limit. The author has had the pleasure of driving this car around Europe, and recalls the ease with which miles were dispatched with fondness. Seven-leaf rear springs, and anti-roll bar up front and telescopic dampers all round keep the car planted on the corners with servo-assisted Ford-based vented disc brakes and snappy throttle response giving a real sense of lightness to the controls. Fifteen-inch Minilite-style 5½-inch wide wheels with grippy Yokohama tyres keep the car wonderfully controllable, the relatively low profile of the tyres prevents the sidewall wobble prevalent on some of the other cars here, while the Ford KA seats fitted front and rear offer great comfort.

Tom Morris's 1961 convertible came alive on mountain roads in the Pyrenees thanks to its perky 1275 A+ engine.

Graphite Grey 15-inch Minilite wheels and matching grille give this Clipper Blue convertible real visual appeal.

Another twist on the concealed indicator theme. Re-purposed front sidelights conceal orange bulbs.

15-inch wheels fill the arches very nicely indeed, despite low-profile rubber.

1963 MORRIS MINOR *1275* SALOON

Technical Specifications

Engine: 1275 MG Midget A-series
Camshaft: Standard MG Midget
Carburettor: HS4
Exhaust: 1.5-inch 'big bore'
Manifold: 1.5-inch cast aluminium inlet, LCB tubular exhaust manifold
Gearbox: Type-9 Ford Five-speed
Ancillaries: Alternator conversion; electronic ignition; electric cooling fan
Suspension: Spax coil overs on front with anti-roll bar; telescopic dampers on rear with seven-leaf Traveller springs and lowering blocks
Differential: 4.22:1
Brakes: Marina-based disc brake conversion (front) with servo assistance

Wheels and tyres: 14in Minilite alloy wheels, 165/80R14
Event MJ683

Impressions

Bought as a daily drive by current owner Andy Wilson, founder member of the Morris Minor Owners Club's Young Members Register, in 2008, this Minor has covered over 60,000 miles in his ownership, travelling as far afield as Austria and Italy.

Fitted with a 1275 MG Midget engine with single HS4 carburettor, it pulls well while remaining relatively understressed, with the fifth gear from the type-9 making cruising relaxed. The coil-over suspension fitted gives this car a far sportier feel around the corners than any of the other cars here, and despite its lowered ride height there are no bangs and crashes over potholes familiar to the author's experience of other lowered Minors, thanks to the additional support of the assister springs.

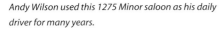

Andy Wilson used this 1275 Minor saloon as his daily driver for many years.

Discreetly positioned aftermarket indicators hide below the rear bumper.

Coil-assisted front dampers keep the car very well planted in the bends.

Owner Andy has driven over 60,000 miles (96,560km) in this Minor.

Numerous lighting upgrades have been made to this car over the years for daily use, including halogen headlights, LED side and brake lights, a high-level brake light and additional indicators. Again the interior is from a Ford KA, while this car also benefits from a two-speed heater from a Mini, head-up GPS speedometer display and a beautiful Moto Lita steering wheel which offers great feel. This is a Minor which has evolved to be a truly great long-distance cruiser and regular user.

THE ULTIMATE IN EVERYDAY MODIFICATIONS?

Each of these cars is exceptional in its own right, and each and every one has been built to fulfil the wants and needs of its owner. There is a specification missing here, though, and it is a specification that several of the 1275, 5-speed gearbox-equipped cars previously described have been through before reaching their current incarnations. It is also one which the author and others here agree is the sweet spot

for Minor modifications. This 'ultimate' in budget-conscious mods keeps the character of the Minor intact while giving it an edge for everyday use and is specified as follows:

A post-'62 Minor with its improved lighting and 1098cc engine. It is fitted with either an HS4 or HIF38 carburettor, 1.5-inch exhaust with long centre branch tubular manifold, its original ribbed case gearbox and a 3.9:1 final drive. Seven-leaf springs at the back, a slight drop of ride height at the front and an anti-roll bar to stiffen things back up. Disc brakes up front to arrest the inevitable extra pace and that is about it.

What is described above can easily be achieved in a number of instalments without the need for heavy lifting or much in terms of parts sourcing or messing around with engines and gearboxes of unknown conditions. The car is capable of cruising at a steady 65mph (105km/h) thanks to the taller final drive and powerful enough for this not to blunt acceleration, thanks to the larger carburettor and exhaust. It is, arguably, the perfect compromise.

Index